To Jack,
  Wishing you every blessing on your special vocation from Lois & John.
                    1994.

Godspells

Also by John Prickett:

Living Stones, British Council of Churches
The Place of Imagination in Religious Education
British Council of Churches

GODSPELLS

John Prickett

The Book Guild Ltd
Sussex, England

This book is sold subject to the condition that it shall not, by way of trade or otherwise, be lent, re-sold, hired out, photocopied or held in any retrieval system or otherwise circulated without the publisher's prior consent in any form of binding or cover other than that in which this is published and without a similar condition including this condition being imposed on the subsequent purchaser.

The Book Guild Ltd
25 High Street,
Lewes, Sussex

First published 1992
© John Prickett 1992

Set in Baskerville by
Raven Typesetters, Ellesmere Port, South Wirral

Printed in Great Britain by
Antony Rowe Ltd.
Chippenham, Wiltshire.

A catalogue record for this book is
available from the British Library

ISBN 0 86332 7281

CONTENTS

List of illustrations   8
Preface   10
Acknowledgements   12

I
WAITING ON GOD

1. The 'Milieu Divin'   17
2. The Supernatural   21
3. Waiting on God   26
4. Silence   30
5. No Longer Mine   34
6. Prayer   38
7. Contemplation   42

II
THE CHRIST

8. Love of God for us   49
9. Love Towards God   55
10. Incarnation   59
11. The Christ   63
12. Death   68
13. Resurrection   72
14. Salvation/Newness of Life   77

III
MEANS OF GRACE

15.	Beauty	85
16.	Truth	90
17.	The Church	95
18.	The Bible	100
19.	Sacrament	106
20.	Sin	110
21.	Judgement	116
22.	Forgiveness	120
23.	Grace	124

IV
LOVE

24.	Faith	131
25.	Humility	137
26.	Obedience	141
27.	Love of Neighbour	145
28.	Human Love/Spiritual Love	149
29.	Love of Enemies	155
30.	Joy	160
31.	World Peace – Reconciliation	165

V
SELF-OFFERING

32.	Friendship	173
33.	Generosity	177
34.	Gratitude	181
35.	Risk	184
36.	The Vulnerable	187
37.	Suffering	191
38.	Fortitude	196

VI
MATURITY

39.	Spontaneity	203
40.	The Greatness of Small Actions	208
41.	Learning/Maturity	212
42.	Freedom	217
43.	Political Holiness	224
44.	The Present Moment	229
45.	Western Civilisation	234
46.	Science and Religion	240
47.	Different Faiths	248
48.	A Catholic (Ecumenical) Spirit	253
49.	Hope	257
50.	Life	261
Biblical References		268
Index of Authors		271

LIST OF ILLUSTRATIONS

In Memoriam		Angel	9
Section	1	Fish in water	18
	2	Bird in wind	24
	5	Hunter's dog	35
	6	Goatsherd	38
	7	Butterfly	43
	8	Bright wings	51
		Hen and chicks	54
	9	The hart	57
	13	Caterpillars and moth	74
	14	Bee gathering honey	77
	15	The rose	88
	18	The Bible	101
		The Vine	103
	19	Chalice	109
	23	Wheat growing	124
		Sparrows	126
	24	Tree rooted and grounded	136
	25	Shrew	140
	26	The elephant	142
	27	Tree of life	148
	30	Racing lambs	163
	31	Dove	169
	33	Abraham	180
	36	Dinosaur	187
	39	Bird singing	205
		Spider, dog and cat	206
	42	Thistledown	223
	44	Poppies	231
	49	The lakeside	258
	50	No Flower	263
		Lilies	265
		The toad	266
Endpiece:		Angel	267

In Memoriam

*B.P.   T.W.P.
W.H.B.   W.E.P.
N.E.P.
J.E.P.
all of whom contributed indirectly
to this book*

*and
Kenneth Macdonald
Killed over Korea May 14, 1952*

PREFACE

This collection is based on a commonplace book which I have kept since I was an undergraduate and contains extracts from those writers who have spoken most tellingly to my heart and mind over a major part of my life.

A 'spell' is something that fascinates: when we are 'spellbound' our attention is fully absorbed in what we contemplate. It is in that sense that these quotations from writers ancient and modern have for me proved to be 'Godspells'. It is my hope that they may be so for others.

It was my original intention to allow the quotations to speak for themselves, but friends have suggested that some comment would be helpful. There is always the danger the comment may inhibit the reader's own response or appear to be condescending. That is a risk I have taken with some reluctance.

While I regard this collection as basically Christian, it includes quotations from other faiths and in some sections suggests ways to a greater mutual understanding through a readiness to listen and learn from each other.

I have tried to balance the mystical element in religion, the religion of the heart, with the asceticism of the mind. Poets and theologians, both have their contribution to make in helping us to find our direction in our search for the Ineffable which always lies beyond our grasp, yet graciously comes to meet us. If this collection helps others, as it has helped me, to find their way in life's journey, I shall be richly rewarded.

I am grateful to my friends Percy Coleman, Patrick Evans, Kenneth Cracknell and Elisabeth Hunkin for reading the manuscript and making valuable suggestions: also to Eva Luxton, Beverley Marston and Frances Cerullo for typing and retyping with evident interest in the material with which they were dealing.

Without the sensitive wood engravings of Sister Margaret

Tournour the book would have lacked much of its attractive appearance; for the way she has worked to meet deadlines in the face of serious health problems I owe her a deep debt of gratitude.

J.P.

ACKNOWLEDGEMENTS & PERMISSIONS

Walter M. Abbot & Very Rev. Msgr. Joseph Gallagher, *The Documents of Vatican II*, Geoffrey Chapman, a division of Cassell Plc; W. H. Auden, *Collected Poems*, 1976, Faber & Faber; D. M. Baillie, *God was in Christ*, Faber & Faber; John Austin Baker, *The Foolishness of God*, 1990, Darton, Longman & Todd Ltd.; Ian Barbour, *Issues in Science and Religion*, 1966, SCM Press; *Believing in the Church*, SPCK, London; William Bloom, *The New Age*; Leonardo Boff, *Church: Charism and Power*, 1985, SCM Press; Dietrich Bonhoeffer, *Life Together*, SCM Press, *The Confessing Church*, SCM Press, *The Cost of Discipleship*, 1948, SCM Press; Ladislaus Boros, *Open Spirit*, 1974, Search Press Ltd.; Fiona Bowie and Oliver Davies, *Hildegard of Bingen, An Anthology*, 1990, SPCK, London; Marcus Braybrooke, *Time to Meet*, 1990, SCM Press; Dr Jacob Bronowski, *The Ascent of Man*, 1973, with permission of BBC Enterprises Ltd.; Peter Brown, *Augustine of Hippo*, 1967, Faber & Faber Ltd.; Herbert Butterfield, *History and Human Relations*, 1951, Collins Publishers, *Christianity and History*, 1949, G. Bell & Sons Ltd.; Owen Chadwick, *Michael Ramsey, A Life*, Oxford University Press; *Concise Dictionary of Religious Quotations*, compiled by William Neil, 1975, Mowbray & Co. Ltd.; C. A. Coulson, *Science and Christian Belief*, 1958, Fontana Books; Kenneth Cracknell, *Towards a New Relationship*, 1986, Epworth Press; Mary Craig, *Candles in the Dark*, 1984, Hodder & Stoughton Ltd.; Kenneth Cragg, *Alive to God*, 1970, *Mind of the Qur'an*, Oxford University Press; Don Cupitt, *Radicals and the Future of the Church*, 1989, SCM Press; Anthony de Mello, *Sadhana, A Way to God*, © 1978, Anthony de Mello S. J., Poona, India, Doubleday, *The Song of the Bird* © 1982, Anthony de Mello S. J., Lonavia, India; *A Dictionary of Christian Spirituality*, ed. by Gordon S. Wakefield, 1983, SCM Press; C. H. Dodd, *The Authority of the Bible*, 1948, James Nisbet & Co. Ltd.; Alan Ecclestone, *The Night Sky of the Lord*, 1980, Darton, Longman & Todd Ltd.; T. S. Eliot, *The Rock*, 1934, *Little Gidding*, *Journey of the Magi*, *Murder in the Cathedral*, 1936, *A Game of Chess*, Faber & Faber; Charles Elliott, *Praying the Kingdom*, 1985, Darton, Longman & Todd Ltd.; Matthew Fox, *Meditations with Meister Eckhart*, 1983, Bear & Co. Inc., *Original Blessing*, 1983, Bear & Co. Inc.; Erich Fromm, *The Fear of Freedom*, 1960, Routledge, *The Art of Loving*; Fynn, *Mister God This is Anna*, 1974, HarperCollins Publishers; Victor Gollancz, *A Year of Grace*, 1955, Victor Gollancz; Dom Bede Griffiths, *The Golden String*, 1979, HarperCollins Publishers; Ronald Grimsley, *Kierkegaard*; David Grossman, *See Under: Love*, Jonathan Cape; Dag Hammarskjöld, *Markings*, 1964, Faber & Faber; Professor Adrian Hastings, *In the Hurricane*, 1986; Vaclav Havel, *Living in Truth*, © Jan Vadislav, 1986, Faber & Faber; John Hick, *God in the Universe of Faiths*, © John Hick, 1988, Macmillan Ltd.; Leonard Hodgson, *The Doctrine of Atonement*, James Nisbet & Co. Ltd.; J. L. Houlden, *Patterns of Faith*, 1977, SCM Press; Gerard Hughes, *God of Surprises*, 1983, Darton, Longman & Todd Ltd.; Aldous Huxley, *The Perennial Philosophy*, 1947, Chatto & Windus; Eric James, *A Life of Bishop John A. T. Robinson*, 1987, HarperCollins Publishers; Daniel Jenkins, *Beyond Religion*, 1962, SCM Press; C. G. Jung, *Modern Man in Search of a Soul*, Routledge, *The Integration of the Personality*, Routledge; Klaus Klostermaier, *Hindu and Christian in Urindaban*; Arthur Koestler, *The Sleepwalkers*, 1959, Hutchinson, permission granted by Peters, Fraser and Dunlop Ltd.;

Hendrik, Kraemer, *The Christian Message in a Non-Christian World*, Edinburgh House Press; Hans Küng, *Does God Exist?* © Hans Küng, 1978, English Translation © 1978, 1979, 1980, HarperCollins Publishers, London and Doubleday & Co., New York, *Eternal Life*, © Hans Küng 1982, English Translation © 1984, HarperCollins Publishers, London and Doubleday & Co., New York, *On Being a Christian*, © Hans Küng 1974, English Translation © 1976, HarperCollins Publishers, London and Doubleday & Co., New York, *Christianity and the World Religions*, © Hans Küng 1985, English Translation © Harper-Collins Publishers, London and Doubleday & Co., New York; Primo Levi, *The Mirror Maker*, Mandarin; T. Lyon, *The Theory of Religious Liberty in England 1603-1639*, 1937, Cambridge University Press; John Main, *The Way of Unknowing*, © 1989, The Executors of John Main OSB, Darton, Longman & Todd Ltd.; Gabriel Marcel, *Being and Having*, translated by Katherine Farrer, Dacre Press; André Maurois, *A History of France*, 1956, Jonathan Cape; Rabbi Meir, in *A Short Survey of the Literature of Rabbinical and Mediaeval Judaism*, W. O. E. Oesterley and A. H. Box, SPCK, London; Hugh Montefiore, *The Probability of God*, 1985, SCM Press; Gabriel Moran, *God Still Speaks*, 1966, Burns & Oates Ltd.; C. F. D. Moule, *The Origin of Christology*, 1977, Cambridge University Press; Iris Murdoch, *The Sovereignty of Good*, 1970, Routledge; Lesslie Newbigin, *The Household of God*, 1953, SCM Press, *The Other Side of 1984*, 1983, World Council of Churches, Geneva, *Christian Freedom in the Modern World*; Donald Nicholl, *Holiness*, 1981, Darton, Longman & Todd Ltd.; Andrew Norman, *Silence in God*, 1990, SPCK, London; Henri Nouwen, *Seeds of Hope*, Darton, Longman & Todd Ltd.; *The Oxford Book of Christian Verse*, chosen and edited by Lord David Cecil, 1940, Oxford University Press; *The Oxford Book of Prayer*, introduction and compilation by George Appleton, 1985, Oxford University Press; *The Oxford Book of Twentieth Century Verse*, chosen by Philip Larkin, 1973, Oxford University Press; *The Oxford Illustrated History of Christianity*, edited by John McManners, 1990, Oxford University Press; Lotte and Werner Pelz, *God is No More*, 1963, Victor Gollancz; Max Plowman, *An Introduction to the Study of Blake*, 1927, J. M. Dent; John Polkinghorne, *The Way the World Is*, 1983, SPCK, London; Stephen Prickett, *Words and the Word*, 1986, Cambridge University Press, *Coleridge and Wordsworth*, 1970, Cambridge University Press; Gerald Priestland, *Priestland's Progress*, 1981, with permission of BBC Enterprises Ltd.; Karl Rahner, *Opportunities for Faith*, 1974, SPCK, London; Michael Ramsey, *Gateway to God*, Darton, Longman & Todd Ltd., *The Gospel and the Catholic Church*, Darton, Longman & Todd Ltd.; Edward Robinson, *The Language of Mystery*, 1987, SCM Press; John A. T. Robinson, *Honest to God*, 1963, SCM Press, *The Priority of John*, 1985, SCM Press; Oscar Romero, *The Church is All of You*, 1984, Chicago Province of the Society of Jesus; Bertrand Russell, *Autobiography*, 1967, HarperCollins Publishers, *What I Believe*, 1925, Routledge; Sankey, Sullivan, Watson, *At Home on Planet Earth*, 1988, The Farmington Trust, Basil Blackwell Ltd.; Edward Schillebeeckx, *Jesus*, © Edward Schillebeeckx, 1974, English Translation © 1979, HarperCollins Publishers, London and Seabury Press, New York, *Christ*, 1980, SCM Press, *God Among Us*, © Uitgeverij H. Nelissen B.V., 1982, Translation © John Bowden 1983, SCM Press; Robin Tanner, *Double Harness*, Impact Books; John V. Taylor, *The Go-Between God*, 1972, SCM Press; Teilhard de Chardin, *On Suffering*, © 1974, Editions du Seuil, English Translation © HarperCollins Publishers, London 1975, *On Love*, © 1967, Editions du Seuil, English Translation © HarperCollins Publishers, London 1972, *Hymn of the Universe*, © 1961, Editions du Seuil, English Translation © HarperCollins Publishers, London 1965; Dylan Thomas, *Selected Works*, © 1976 by Trustees of the copyrights of the late Dylan Thomas, J. M. Dent; R. S. Thomas, *Selected Poems 1946-1968*, © R. S. Thomas 1946, 1952, 1953, 1955, 1958, 1961, 1963, 1966, 1968, 1973, Granada Publishing; Paul Tillich, *The Shaking of the Foundations*, 1949, SCM Press, *Christianity and the Encounter of the World Religions* (publisher untraced); Paul Tournier, *The Strong and the Weak*, 1963, SCM Press; Philip Toynbee, *Towards Holy Spirit*, 1973, SCM Press; Jennifer Uglow, *George Eliot*, 1987, Virago Press; Laurens van der Post, *A Walk with a White Bushman*, 1986, The Hogarth Press; W. H. Vanstone, *Love's Endeavour, Love's Expense*, 1977, Darton, Longman & Todd Ltd.; Stephen Verney, *Water into Wine*, 1985, HarperCollins Publishers; Keith Ward, *A Vision to Pursue*, 1991, SCM Press; Neville Ward, *Five for Sorrow, Ten for*

Joy, 1971, Epworth Press, *Friday Afternoon*, 1976, Epworth Press; Patrick White, *Riders in the Chariot*, 1961, © the estate of Patrick White, Jonathan Cape; Victor White, *God and the Unconscious*, 1953, The Harvill Press; H. A. Williams, *True Resurrection*, 1972, *The True Wilderness*, 1965, © H. A. Williams, in *Soundings*, 1962, Cambridge University Press; Danah Zohar, *The Quantum Self*, 1990, Bloomsbury Publishing Ltd.

All Darton, Longman and Todd and Oxford University Press publications mentioned above are used by permission of the publishers; William Bloom, *The New Age*, 1991, Rider; Rex Brico, *Brother Roger and His Community*, 1978; Ronald Grimsley, *Kirkdgaard*, London, Studio Vista; prayer from Oxford Book of Prayer, reprinted from *Journey of a Soul*, Collins; Dorothy Sayers, *Unpopular Opinions*, London, 1951; Tillich, *The Shaking of the Foundations*, 1949, SCM Press; Gordon S. Wakefield, article on spirituality in the *Dictionary of Christian Spirituality*, 1983, SCM Press; Leslie D. Weatherhead, *The Christian Agnostic*, 1965, Hodder and Stoughton Ltd.; Vidler, ed., *Soundings*, Cambridge University Press; *The Mind of the Kur'an*, Allen & Unwin, 1973; *Toads* by Philip Larkin from *The Less Deceived*, 1955, reprinted by permission of the Marbell Press, England, Primo Levi, *The Mirror Maker*, Methuen, London.

Extracts have been quoted from the following editions and translated by the author:
Albert Camus, *La Chute*, 1956, Gallimard; Françoise Chandernagor, *La Sans Pareille*, Editions de Fallois, 1988; Raissa Maritain, *Les Grandes Amitiés* (edition untraced); Antoine de Saint-Exupéry, *Pilote de Guerre*, Gallimard, 1942, *Terre des Hommes*, Hachette, 1956; Teilhard de Chardin, *Le Milieu Divin*, Editions du Seuil; Simone Weil, *Attente de Dieu*, Editions du Vieux Colombier, 1950, *La Pesanteur et la Grâce*, Librairie Plon, 1948.

THE BIBLE

Quotations from *The Jerusalem Bible* (JB), published and copyright 1966, 1967, 1968, by Darton, Longman & Todd Ltd., and Doubleday & Co. Inc., are used by the permission of the publishers.

Quotations from the *New English Bible* (NEB), Second Edition © 1970, are used by permission of Oxford and Cambridge University Presses.

Scripture quotations from the *Holy Bible, New International Version* (NIV), © 1973, 1978, 1984, are used by permission of the International Bible Society.

Scripture quotations from the *Revised Standard Version of the Bible* (RSV) © 1971 and 1952 are used by permission of the Division of Christian Education of the National Council of the Churches of Christ in the U.S.A.

Extracts from the *Book of Common Prayer* of 1662 (BCP), the rights in which are vested in the Crown in perpetuity with the United Kingdom, are reproduced by permission of the Crown's patentee, Cambridge University Press.

Extracts from the *Authorized Version of the Bible* (The King James Bible) (AV), the rights in which are vested in the Crown, are reproduced by permission of the Crown's patentee, Cambridge University Press.

Extracts from *The Living Bible* (LB), © 1971, are used by permission of Kingsway Publications, Eastbourne.

Extracts from *Forms of Prayer for Jewish Worship* (FPJW) are published with the permission of Rabbi Hugo Gryn, West London Synagogue of British Jews.

The author gratefully acknowledges quotations from *The Times*, *The Spectator*, *The Independent*, *Theology*, *Concilium*, *R.E. Today*, *The Farmington Trust Occasional Papers*, *Audenshaw Papers*, and from B.B.C. broadcasts by Bishop Richard Harries, Rabbi Hugo Gryn, Joseph Campbell and Indarjit Singh, all of which are detailed in the Index.

When the author began to make this collection many years ago, he had no intention of publishing and did not always record sources. In some cases, it has not proved possible to trace the source of a quotation and for these he offers his apology to the authors or copyright holders.

Passages printed in italics are comment by the author.

I
WAITING ON GOD

1

THE 'MILIEU DIVIN'

> Beyond; beyond, and yet again beyond'
> What went ye out to seek, oh foolish fond?
> Is not the heart of all things here and now?
> Is not the circle infinite and the centre
> Everywhere, if ye would but hear and enter?
> *Alfred Noyes*

The 'Milieu Divin', immense as it is, is in fact a Centre. It has, then, the properties of a centre, that is to say, above all, the absolute and ultimate power to reunite (and consequently to bring to fulfilment) all existence in its heart. In the Milieu Divin all the elements of the universe touch each other at their most positive and inward point. Little by little they concentrate there, without loss and without subsequent danger of corruption, all that is most pure and attractive in them. On the other hand they lose, in meeting, the mutual outwardness and the barriers to mutual understanding which are the deepest afflictions of human relationships.

Teilhard de Chardin

A dissipated man is a man that is separated from God; that is, disunited from his centre; whether this be occasioned by hurry of business, by seeking honour or preferment, or by fondness for diversions . . . The dissipated life is not barely that of a powdered beau, or a petit-maitre, a gamester, a woman-hunter, a playhouse-hunter, a fox-hunter, or a shatterbrain of any kind; but the life of an honourable statesman, a gentleman, or a merchant that is 'without God in the world'.

John Wesley

Let us make our home in the Milieu Divin. Then we shall find ourselves in touch with what is most intimate in souls and what is most stable in matter. There, where all beauty flows together, we shall discover the most vital, the most sensitive and the most active point of the universe. At the same time we shall find that at the heart of our being, our powers of action and of adoration are effortlessly deployed in all their fullness.

Nor need the Christian fear that in plunging into deep waters he will lose his foothold in the Revelation and the Life . . . To his sensitive eyes, it is true, the Creator, and more precisely the Redeemer, are immerged and spread abroad in things to the point where, in the words of Saint Angèle de Foligno 'the world is full of God'. But this expansion has value in his eyes only so far as the light, in which for him all things are bathed, shines from an historical base and is transmitted along a quite definite traditional axis.

Teilhard de Chardin

Every moment is the message of God's will; every external event, everything outside us, and even every involuntary thought and feeling within us is God's own touch. We are living in touch with God. Everything we come in contact with, the whole of our daily circumstances, and all our interior responses, whether pleasures or pains, are God's working. We are living in God – in God's action, as a fish in the water. There is no question of trying to feel that God is here, or to complain of God being far, once He has taught us that we are bathed in Him, in His action in His will.

Dom John Chapman

There appears to be no satisfactory translation of the French words Milieu Divin. *The literal meaning of 'Milieu' is 'middle'. In Fynn's book* Mr. God, This is Anna, *Anna speaks of God as 'In my Middle'. 'Milieu' can also mean 'environment', material or social. John Chapman writes, 'We are living in God, in God's action, as a fish in the water'. The water is the 'Milieu' in which the fish lives.*

The life of every moment is a phenomenon of God's heart. Every task is the combustion of the flame of God. He greets us in the kitchen. He gazes intently upon us at the well-curb. In the bustle and hustle of the factory or when hanging on the strap in the crowded car we breathe God. When we lift the iron sledge and are hammering out the steel we are in God's bosom.

This is the mood of the true soul: to be drunk, not with liquor but with God. To feast to one's heart's content, not on food but on God. In dreaming and in waking hours, in sorrow and in laughter, to walk in a world flooded with light, this is a phenomenon experienced only by those who truly know the soul's art.

Toyohito Kagawa

God cannot be used as a stop-gap. We must not wait until we are at the end of our tether: He must be found at the centre of life: in life, and not only in death; in health and vigour, and not only in suffering; in activity and not only in sin. The ground for this lies in the revelation of God in Christ.

Dietrich Bonhoeffer

Professor Himmelfarb . . . was racked by his persistent longing to exceed the bounds of reason: to gather up the sparks, visible intermittently inside the thick shells of human faces; to break through to the sparks of light imprisoned in the forms of wood and stone. Imperfection in himself had enabled him to recognise the fragmentary nature of things, but at the same time restrained him from undertaking the immense labour of reconstruction. So this imperfect man had remained necessarily tentative. He was for ever peering into bushes or windows, or the holes of eyes, or, with his stick, testing the thickness of a stone, as if in search of further evidence when he should have been gathering up the infinitesimal kernels of sparks, which he already knew to exist and planting them again in the bosom of divine fire, from which they had been let fall in the beginning.

Patrick White

Christianity alone safeguards, together with the rights of the mind, the essential aspiration of every mystic: to become one with the Other while remaining oneself.

Teilhard de Chardin

For me the ultimate context in which life is lived is that of an I–Thou relationship with the Eternal Thou. That relationship is the umbilical cord of all that one is and all that one does . . . It is not something that begins and ends with what we call time, but it is the framework in which all things of space and time belong and are created and have their being. It is defined in Christ in terms of the love of God and fellowship and grace. It is the centre of everything and it is the context in which one tries to face everything else.

John A. T. Robinson

In him we live, and move, and have our being.

Acts 17:28

2

THE SUPERNATURAL

What gives life to a physical organism is something which does not proceed from it but which is above it: and, analogously, what gives happiness in life to a human being is something which does not proceed from human nature but which is above human nature.

Augustine of Hippo

In our day more than ever before the Church needs to hear the testimony that God is beyond all things, beyond all attempts to define him in thought or word or to reach him by activity. The Church has need of an inner silence that her word may be significant, of a suspension of activity that her work may be fruitful, and of that which is beyond – all – sign so that she may reach the fulness of the sacramental sign which she herself is.

Abishikta Nanda

This four dimensional war not only threatens the civil guarantees won in the past century and a half; it raises the question whether the liberation of man from allegiance to a higher, absolute authority, gradually effected in the course of three and a half centuries of enlightenment, was right. It has revealed the limitations of an entirely earth-bound philosophy. For men are only humane when they do not make themselves and their aims the centre of their system, but subordinate it to that which is higher than man. Humanism is thus the first step toward dehumanisation, because it makes man his own judge and himself the end and aim of life, recognizing no judgement of a transcendental authority.

Rauschning

The centre of me is always and eternally a terrible pain – a curious wild pain – a searching for something beyond what the world contains, something transfigured and infinite – the beatific vision – God – I do not find it, I do not think it is to be found – but the love of it is my life – it's like passionate love for a ghost. At times it fills me with rage, at times with wild despair, it is the source of gentleness and cruelty and work, it fills every passion that I have – it is the actual spring of life within me.
Bertrand Russell

Hoimar von Ditfurth is right when he argues that evolution itself has opened our eyes to the fact that reality cannot end at the point where our experience of reality comes to an end: 'that the range of the real world must transcend quantitatively and qualitatively by inconceivable dimensions the horizon of knowledge available to us at the present level of development.'
Hans Küng

I am amazed at the audacity with which some people speak about God.
Blaise Pascal

It is our traditional belief about the gods, and we can see it in our experience of men, that by natural necessity, every being exerts to the full all the power at its disposal.' (Thucydides.) That is not true of the God of the Christians. He is a supernatural God whereas Jehovah is a natural God.
Simone Weil

From all bodies together we cannot obtain one little thought; this is impossible, and of another order. From all bodies and minds, we cannot produce a feeling of true charity; this is impossible and of another and supernatural order.
Blaise Pascal

Europe received from it (Christianity) a drift which had hitherto been unknown to it – it learnt the fundamental truth that life cannot be an end-in-itself, but that the true end of our existence lies beyond it.
Arthur Schopenhauer

The sense of a Reality beyond human kind appears to be universal, even in an unbeliever like Bertrand Russell, for whom the search for 'something beyond what the world contains' is 'the actual spring of life within me'. Roger Schutz, having found what Bertrand Russell only sought despairingly, expresses his finding in a down-to-earth manner:

Some people ask me for autographs or other nonsense of that sort. I tell them that a Christian cannot agree with expressions focussing upon himself and not on the one Reality that matters. I am a humble servant and I will remain so until my dying day.

Simone Weil makes the important distinction between an anthropomorphic God, made in the image of man, and a supernatural God not conceivable by the natural man, but revealed from a supernatural Source.

John Robinson (in Honest to God*) was concerned to find a way of expressing transcendence acceptable to 20th century man.*

I have an immense respect for the boundary walls of human awareness. I know these walls are finite, but at the same time I know they are not opaque. There is a very strange light coming through them. But most of all there are strange events that come over these walls that I cannot explain and that I cannot ignore. I just accept them and they prove to me how great the area of unknowing is outside, and how important it is for our own increase not to reject it but just to allow the sense of mystery and wonder it evokes to preside over one's imagination. There is a dynamic reality beyond the here and the now.
Laurens Van der Post

I was concerned not to abolish transcendence (for without transcendence God becomes indistinguishable from the world, and so superfluous), but to find a way of expressing transcendence which would not tie God's reality to a supranaturalistic or mythological world-view which, if not actually falsifying, was largely meaningless for twentieth-century man.
John A.T. Robinson

At times I feel like one of those birds one sees blown around at the mercy of a high wind.

> Spiritual forces are so much more powerful
> and mysterious than those of Matter.
> *Teilhard de Chardin*

We could say that, for all the complex historical detours, the origin of the modern state and of modern political power may be sought precisely here, that is once again in a moment when human reason begins to 'free' itself from the human being as such, from his personal experience, personal conscience and personal responsibility and so also from that to which, within the framework of the natural world, all responsibility is uniquely related, his absolute horizon.

Vaclav Havel

Responsibility for and towards words is a task which is intrinsically ethical. As such, however, it is situated beyond the horizon of the visible world, in that realm wherein dwells the Word that was in the beginning and is not the word of Man.

Vaclav Havel

I cannot define for you what God is. I can only say that my work has proved empirically that the pattern of God exists in every man, and that this pattern has at its disposal the greatest of all energies for transformation and transfiguration of his natural being.

C.G. Jung

Why had I needed to search so long? Why had I expected a teaching that would come from outside myself? Why had I expected the world to justify itself to me, and prove its meaning and purity? It was for me to justify the world by loving and forgiving it, to discover its meaning through love, to purify it through forgiveness . . .

What name was I to use? 'God', I murmured, 'God'. How else would I address Him. O Universe? O Heap? O Whole? As 'Father' or 'Mother'? . . .

'Thou' is His name, to which 'God' may be added. For 'I' and 'me' are no more than a pause between the immensity of the universe which is Him and the very depth of our self, which is also Him.

Petru Dumitrio

The New Age movement represents several very different dynamics, but they thread together to communicate the same message: there is an invisible and inner dimension to all life – cellular, human and cosmic. The most exciting work in the world is to explore this inner reality.

William Bloom

> Watch with me, inward solemn influence,
> Invisible, intangible, unkenned;
> Wind of the darkness that shall bear me hence;
> O life within my life, flame within flame,
> Who mak'st me one with song that has no end,
> And with that stillness whence my spirit came.
>
> *Siegfried Sassoon*

3

WAITING ON GOD

Only God himself can turn away his own judgements upon his people. For ruined Jerusalem nothing remains but to trust God ... If a man set to work without any special call or commission, to build the ruined Church up again, it would be a defiance of God's judgement. And this would be so however virtuous the intention, however pure the teaching, however deep the pastoral concern for the people. This is the way that impertinent carnal piety would act, but not the faith of God's community. Faith waits and bows before the judgement, till God himself returns: it waits and prays for the awakening.

Dietrich Bonhoeffer

A man may be of value to another man, not because he wishes to be important, not because he possesses some inner wealth of soul, not because of something he is, but because of what he is – not. His importance may consist in his poverty, in his hopes and fears, in his waiting and hurrying, in the direction of his whole being to what lies beyond his horizon and beyond his power. The importance of an apostle is negative rather than positive. In him a void becomes visible.

Karl Barth

Man attains in religion, as truly as elsewhere – once given his wholehearted striving – in proportion as he seeks not too directly, not feverishly and strainingly, but in a largely subconscious, waiting, genial, expansive, endlessly patient, sunny manner.

Von Hügel

What I am trying, with some difficulty, to identify and describe here is that capacity we have . . . for launching ourselves into an action without having a clear and distinct idea of what precisely the end will be. It is the ability to remain in this state of suspended expectation, and to maintain it through long periods of concentrated activity, that is characteristic of all truly creative achievement.
Edward Robinson

To transform the creation man has to be active and extrovert, but to be transformed by the Creator he has to be broken and still before God. To keep these two aspects of existence together is the demand of the time from God and History.
Paul Verghese

I am convinced that much of the rebellion against Christianity is due to the overt or veiled claim of the Christian to possess God, and therefore, also, to the loss of this element of waiting, so decisive for the prophets and the apostles . . . they did not possess God: they waited for Him . . . Is God less than a human person? We always have to wait for a human being.
Paul Tillich

There is a well known hymn which begins, 'Rise up, O men of God!'; it is a call to action and service. No doubt such a call is at times appropriate; it is stirring, like a bugle call, but it can be both superficial and impatient. No less urgent at times may be the command, 'Sit down, O men of God! Sit down, and wait!' – not to sleep, but alert and expectant.

> Except the Lord build the house,
> They labour in vain that build it;
> Except the Lord keep the city,
> The watchman waiteth but in vain.
> *Psalm 127:1*

If we wait in hope and patience, the power of that for which we wait is already effective within us . . . We are stronger when we wait than when we possess.
Paul Tillich

Moments of great calm
Kneeling before an altar
of wood in a stone church
In summer, waiting for the God
To speak, the air a staircase
For silence; the sun's light
Ringing me, as though I acted
A great role. And the audience
Still; all that close throng
Of spirits waiting, as I,
For the message.
   Prompt me, God;
But not yet. When I speak,
Though it be you who speak
Through me, something is lost,
The meaning is in the waiting.

R.S. Thomas

I hope in the Lord,
my soul has hope,
and for his word I wait.

My soul waits for the Lord
more than watchmen for the morning,
watching for the morning.

Psalm 130:5,6

Prayer is first of all waiting. It is allowing the 'Come, Lord!' of the Apocalypse to well up in oneself day after day. Come for mankind!. Come for us all! Come for me!

It is not the privilege of a few. It is an easily accessible reality, for tiny children as for the old.

Wait! Wait for the dawn of a life, when God gathers us to Himself for ever. Wait for the spring time of the Church. Wait, in spite of everything, for Christ to transfigure our failures and turn our bitterness into the spirit of mercy, for love which is not consuming fire is not charity.

God is preparing us a new Pentecost which will set every one of us ablaze with the fire of his love.

Roger Schutz

I said to my soul, be still, and wait without hope
For hope would be hope for the wrong thing; wait without love
For love would be love of the wrong thing; there is yet faith
But the faith and the love and the hope are all in the waiting.
Wait without thought, for you are not ready for thought:
So the darkness shall be the light, and the stillness the dancing.
T.S. Eliot

    In the stilled silence
    Mind, heart and soul
    wait upon God
       reach out to God.

    Not thinking
      Not asking
        Not doing
    Just waiting
     stilled
       upon
         God.

St. Mary's Abbey, West Malling

4

SILENCE

Elected Silence sing to me
And beat upon my whorlèd ear
Pipe me to pastures still and be
The music that I care to hear
G.M. Hopkins

Talk of God that does not in the last resort, emerge from silence and lead again into silence does not know with whom it is dealing.
Hans Küng

The eternal silence of these infinite spaces terrifies me.
Blaise Pascal

It is not only the silence of outer space that frightens us: equally frightening is the silence of inner space.

In company a hostess feels an obligation to break an embarrassing silence. Even in church a silence of more than a few seconds is unacceptable. Hindus and Buddhists and Christian monastics have learned how to use silence to look inward, but among Christian denominations only the Quakers have learned how to use it in public worship: Graham and Hoyland were both Quakers:

Contemplation, meditation, collectedness, inward purgation are the very processes of the mystical experiences of the soul. They need an activity of the spirit absolutely blocked by the necessity for attention to other peoples's words.
J.W. Graham

> Ungainly, foolish words
> How can mere words,
> The mask and darkening of reality,
> Express thy Being?
> How can mere words
> Set forth thy praise?
>
> *John S. Hoyland*

Teach me to go to the country beyond words and beyond names.

Thomas Merton

The very best and utmost of attainment in this life is to remain still and let God act and speak in thee.

Meister Eckhart

> The Eagle soars in the summit of Heaven,
> The Hunter with his dogs pursues his circuit
> O perpetual revolution of configured stars,
> O perpetual recurrence of determined seasons,
> O world of spring and autumn, birth and dying
> The endless cycle of idea and action,
> Endless invention, endless experiment,
> Brings knowledge of motion, but not of stillness,
> Knowledge of speech, but not of silence;
> Knowledge of words, and ignorance of the Word.
>
> *T.S. Eliot*

In my medical experience as well as in my own life I have again and again been faced with the mystery of Love, and have never been able to explain what it is. Like Job, I had to 'lay my hand on my mouth. I have spoken once, and I will not answer' (Job 40:4f.). Here is the greatest and smallest, the remotest and nearest, the highest and lowest, and we cannot discuss one side of it without also discussing the other. No language is adequate to this paradox. Whatever one can say, no words express the whole. To speak of partial aspects is always too much or too little, for only the whole is meaningful. Love 'bears all things' and 'endures all things' (1 Cor. 13:7). These words say all there is to be said; nothing can be added to them.

C.G. Jung

> Great things are done when Men
> and Mountains meet;
> This is not done by Jostling
> in the Street.
>
> *William Blake*

Be still and know that I am God.

Psalm 46.v10

Lord teach me to silence my own heart that I may listen to the gentle movement of the Holy Spirit within me and sense the depths which are of God.

(15th Century Frankfurt Prayer)

> She moves in tumult; round her lies
>   The silence of the world of grace;
> The twilight of our mysteries
>   Shines like high noonday on her face;
> Our piteous guesses, dim with fears,
> She touches, handles, sees, and hears.
>
> *Robert Hugh Benson*
> (of a Teresian Contemplative)

There are some things which lose their scent when exposed to the air; there are intimate thoughts which cannot be translated into the language of this earth, without instantly losing their profound and heavenly meaning.

Thérèse of Lisieux

> *Alone* . . . this word is life endured and known.
> It is the stillness where our spirits walk
> And all but inmost faith is overthrown.
>
> *Siegfried Sassoon*

> The longest journey
> Is the journey inwards.
>
> *Dag Hammarskjold*

> Hush, be still,
> Impregnated with silence
> We carry
> The Word
>
> *Andrew Norman*

Nothing in the world is so like God as stillness.
Meister Eckhart

    Be silent
      still
        aware
    For there
    In your own heart
    The spirit is at prayer.
     Listen and learn
       Open and find
         heart wisdom
           Christ.
St. Mary's Abbey, West Malling

5

NO LONGER MINE

Sometimes you say you feel yourself drawn to adore the divine Majesty with humility mixed with love, and by very distinct acts which arise of their own accord apparently, and are very delightful, filling the soul with a great contentment. At other times you are inclined to remain in complete repose with a clear apprehension of the presence of God, and without the power of forming distinct acts, unless with violent efforts . . . It is certain that each of these two states is a gift of God, but the second seems to be the better; first because it is more simple, more profound, more spiritual, and further removed from the senses, consequently, more worthy of God Who is a pure spirit and Whom we must worship in spirit and in truth; secondly because it is an exercise of pure faith, which is less satisfying to the soul, less reassuring, and consequently in which there is more of sacrifice and of perfect abandonment to God. Thirdly, because in this state it is the Holy Spirit that acts with the approval and consent of the soul while in the first state it is the soul that acts with the grace of God.

J. P. de Caussade

St. John of the Cross preaches neither mutilation nor suicide, nor the slightest ontological destruction of the most fragmentary filament of the wing of the smallest gnat. He is not concerned with the structure of our substance and its faculties: he is concerned with our *proprietorship of ourselves*, as expressed in the use we make of our active power as free and morally responsible beings. And there he demands everything of us. There we have to give everything. What he does preach is a very real death, a death much more subtle and delicate than any material death or destruction: the death which is called the *expropriation of the self.* This destruction of self-will is a death which is active and effective within our being, a death which is experienced and freely undergone; it is within the innermost activity of the spirit that it takes place, and by this spirit that it is brought about. It grows with the growth of the spirit, and cleaves to it in its inmost depths. But it is a death which does not destroy sensitivity, but, on the contrary, refines it and makes it more exquisite. It does not harden the fibres of the being, but, on the contrary, makes them supple and spiritualizes them. It is a death which transforms us into love.

Jacques Maritain

Doubtless the essence of our ministry, as it is the duty of every Christian, is to proclaim the Gospel; but that does not mean to transform our neighbour in our way or according to our own particular ideas, for of ourselves we can do nothing, we can only walk before Grace as a dog goes in front of the invisible hunter, with more or less effect, as we are more or less attentive, docile and pliable, in order to become responsive to the will of the Master and indifferent to our own.

François Mauriac

God does not want to be believed in, to be debated and defended by us, but simply to be realized through us.

Martin Buber

Belief in God is the trust, the well-nigh incredible trust, that to give ourselves to the uttermost in love is not to be confounded but to be 'accepted', that Love is the ground of our being, to which ultimately we 'come home'.

John A.T. Robinson

Each of our lives is as it were woven by these two threads: the thread of interior development in which our ideas, affections, human and mystical attitudes are formed; and the thread of outward success by following which we find ourselves, at each moment, at that precise point where all the forces of the Universe will converge to bring to bear upon us the result intended by God.

My God, so that at each moment, you may find me as you wish me to be, in the place where you expect me to be, that is to say, so that you may take full possession of me both by the interior and exterior of my whole being, let me never break this double thread of my life.

Teilhard de Chardin

I feel myself at home in the hands of the Lord and never, perhaps, have I tasted so fully the joy of letting myself fall into the future as when I fall into the depths of his very Being.

Teilhard de Chardin

We sink eternally from letting go to letting go into God.

Meister Eckhart

The real question is not Peace = satisfied feeling, but Peace = willed abandonment.

Evelyn Underhill

Self sacrifice means whole self-giving, an unqualified renunciation of every claim on what we possess – and we do not possess ourselves. Indeed, the more we advance in self-knowledge and self-possession, with or without the aid of psychology the less we find we know, the more we find that is beyond our dominion and control, the more we know we are *not* our own, and therefore are incapable of self-sacrifice. Only a Lord of all, who possesses all, can initiate and consummate the sacrifice, and impart to us the new life that springs from death.

Victor White

Through death to life: 'a death which transforms us into love' (J. Maritain) This is the paradox beyond the grasp of the intellect, yet central to the experience of the spiritual life. Teilhard de Chardin brings together 'two threads' – the outward and the inward aspects of our lives. To be at the right place, at the right time, with the right inward attitude, is to enable God to 'take full possession' of us and to work through us.

. . . we are to abandon ourselves to him every moment, to know that he holds us in being whether or not we hold him in consciousness.

There is no time, nor place, nor situation when we are outside his presence and his love.

Gordon S. Wakefield

One could have predicted the loss of the Via Negativa in the West because of the fact that the Via Positiva and a spirituality of pleasure and hospitality were so profoundly silenced for so long. There is no Via Negativa without a Via Positiva. How can one let go of what one has not fallen in love with? The depth of nothingness is directly related to the experience of everythingness. The void is the convex of the concave surface of the cosmos. We learn we are cosmic beings not only in our joy and ecstasy but also in our pain and sorrow.

Matthew Fox

I am no longer my own, but yours. Put me to what you will, rank me with whom you will; put me to doing, put me to suffering; let me be employed for you or laid aside for you, exalted for you or brought low for you; let me be full, let me be empty; let me have all things, let me have nothing; I freely and wholeheartedly yield all things to your pleasure and disposal.

Methodist Covenant

> A condition of complete simplicity
> Costing not less than everything.

T.S. Eliot

6

PRAYER

For the man whose calling in this world is, for instance, to teach and educate others, prayer will be to see in his children and pupils the mystery of God, which is waiting, as it were, to be brought forth. For him, prayer is to help children to grow up in the knowledge of creation (including all the sciences of earth and of man), as the work of a loving God,

to

admire its

marvels

and

to praise

the Lord

for it:

to help them to grow also in the knowledge of themselves, in the awareness of inner soul, so that they discover deep within themselves the privileged place where God himself is waiting for them.

Abishikta Nanda

Trying to live in depth takes us out of our depth and so creates the sense of need which is the beginning of prayer.

We must wish to have the prayer that God gives us and no other. A distracted prayer, a desolate prayer, a happy prayer – we must take everything as it comes. For our union with God consists in doing and accepting His will, moment by moment all through the day. Nothing else matters.

Dom John Chapman

Above all I recommend to you prayer of the mind and heart, and, above all, that which has for its subject the life and passion of our Lord. For, by beholding Him often in meditation your whole soul will be filled with Him, you will learn His disposition, and you will form your actions after the model of His. He is the light of the world, and therefore it is in Him, by Him, and for Him that we must be enlightened and illumined . . . Believe me we cannot go to God the Father but by this door.

St. Francis de Sales

The 'immediate' person thinks and imagines that when he prays, the important thing, the thing he must concentrate upon, is that God should hear what he is praying for. Yet in the true, eternal sense it is just the reverse: the true relation in prayer is not when God hears what is prayed for, but when the person praying continues to pray until he is the one who hears, who hears what God wills. The 'immediate' person, therefore . . . makes demands in his prayers; the true man of prayer only attends.

Kierkegaard

Prayer, crystallised in words, assigns a permanent wavelength on which the dialogue has to be continued, even when our mind is occupied with other matters.

Dag Hammarskjold

A man should utter daily a hundred Benedictions.
Rabbi Meir

I wonder whether Christian prayer, prayer in the light of the Incarnation, is not to be defined in terms of penetration through the world to God rather than withdrawal from the World to God . . . what enlightenment I have had on decisions has almost always come not when I have gone away and stood back from them, but precisely as I have wrestled through all the most practical pros and cons, usually with other people. And this activity, undertaken by a Christian trusting and expecting that God is there, would seem to be prayer.
John A.T. Robinson

The right relation between prayer and conduct is not that conduct is supremely important and prayer may help it, but that prayer is supremely important and conduct tests is.
William Temple

Lift up your heart to Him, sometimes even at your meals, and when you are in company: the least little remembrance will always be acceptable to Him. You need not cry very loud. He is nearer to us than we are aware of
Brother Lawrence

My ending is despair,
Unless I be reliev'd by prayer.
William Shakespeare

If you came this way,
Taking any route, starting from anywhere,
At any time or at any season,
It would always be the same: you would have to put off
Sense and notion. You are not here to verify,
Instruct yourself, or inform curiosity
Or carry report. You are here to kneel
Where prayer has been valid. And prayer is more
Than an order of words, the conscious occupation
Of the praying mind, or the sound of the voice praying.
And what the dead had no speech for, when living,
They can tell you, being dead: the communication

Of the dead is tongued with fire beyond the language of the living.
T.S. Eliot

In one sense, prayer is a step from doubt towards faith, a creative waiting to perceive in every event the Creator at work today. It is secret wonder and thankfulness for the gift of life.
Roger Schutz

Prayer is the direction towards God of all the attention of which the soul is capable. The quality of attention counts for much in the quality of the prayer. Warmth of heart is no substitute for it.
Simone Weil

There is the kind of prayer in which God is active and we are receptive. This involves the opening of the heart towards God in an attitude of listening and waiting.

Simone Weil thinks of prayer as an act of attention and concentration – something more than warmth of heart. No doubt, as Kierkegaard suggests, the intention is the same: to continue to pray (i.e. to attend) until we hear or, as St. Francis de Sales put it, 'learn his disposition'.

John Robinson sees prayer as more active – a wrestling with problems – but always 'trusting and expecting that God is there'.

There seem to be two levels here – 'the conscious occupation of the praying mind' (T.S. Eliot), and the far deeper 'basic trust' (Hans Küng), which may underlie all conscious effort or activity. Both levels may be involved in prayer, but there can be little doubt which is the more profound and therefore more effective.

This division of the self into two, a top half which is excitable and easily disturbed, and a deeper part that is more real, quieter, wiser and can be fixed on God though the upper part is a revolting mess – this idea has been much used by the saints and ordinary Christians still find it helpful.
J. Neville Ward

Church-bels beyond the stars heard, the soul's bloud,
The land of spices, something understood.
George Herbert

7

CONTEMPLATION

Martha, Martha, you worry and fret about so many things, and yet few are needed, indeed only one. It is Mary who has chosen the better part: it is not to be taken from her.

Luke 10: 41-42

An instant of pure love is more precious in the sight of God and more profitable to the Church than all other good works put together, though it may seem as if nothing were done . . . Let those men of zeal who think by their preaching and exterior works to convert the world, consider that they would be much more pleasing to God - to say nothing of the example they would give – if they would spend at least one half of their time in prayer, even though they may not have attained to unitive love. Certainly they would do more and with less trouble, by one single good work than by a thousand; because of the merit of their prayer and the spiritual strength which it supplies.

St. John of the Cross

I make it my business only to persevere in His holy presence, wherein I keep myself by a simple attention, and a general fond regard to God, which I may call an actual presence of God; or, to speak better, an habitual, silent, and secret conversation of the soul with God . . .

Brother Lawrence

To pray according to your first method is to pray by formal, successive and perceptible acts: to pray according to the second method is to pray by implicit acts, experienced, but in no way expressed nor perceptible except confusedly. Or, in other words it is to pray by a simple but actual inclination of the heart; now this simple and real inclination of the heart contains all, and says all to God without, however, express words . . . it is called a loving waiting on God, a simple looking, or pure faith and simplicity tending to God, arising from the love of God, and producing an ever increasing love of God . . . You will see that this method is of more value than the other; you must, therefore, make it your principal exercise, without however neglecting the first at certain times.

J. P. de Caussade

And what does this little messenger (the butterfly) tell us? Exactly what the prophets proclaimed: that there is a prayer and that this prayer begins with the very first light of every life, that to pray is not to ask that we may receive, but to ask that we may become (the receiving is contained in the becoming), that to contemplate is to keep one's eyes steadily fixed on one's ideal with a regard which never strays from its object, and an unbounded heart which is found only in those who no longer see themselves.

Alphonse de Chateaubriand

Contemplation is described as 'a simple and real inclination of the heart' (de Caussade), 'a simple attention, and a general fond regard to God' (Brother Lawrence). What our writers claim is that this loving waiting on God does more than committee meetings, preaching, and all 'exterior works' to convert the world. This is, of course, the belief of all monastics. For the most part they do not see themselves as separated from the world, but, through their prayer, as actively recreating it. For the active person in the world this is extremely difficult to believe; only experience will convince. For John Main, stillness at the centre and, for Anthony de Mello, wonder, are of the essence of contemplation.

I think there is a place both inside and outside religion for a sort of contemplation of the Good, not just by dedicated experts but

by ordinary people: an attention which is not just the planning of particular good actions but an attempt to look right away from self towards a distant transcendent perfection, a source of uncontaminated energy, a source of *new* and quite undreamt-of virtue. This attempt, which is a turning of attention away from the particular, may be the thing that helps most when difficulties seem insoluble, and especially when feelings of guilt keep attracting the gaze back towards the self. This is the true mysticism which is morality, a kind of undogmatic prayer . . .
Iris Murdoch

When we meditate we do indeed suspend all the separate operations of our being. But not because we reject any one of them. The mind, with all its levels of consciousness, is a wonderful gift which has been given to each of us. Our capacity for rational analysis, the power of imagination and of making distinctions, all these operations are peerless gifts given to us. Similarly, our capacity to enter into relationships with others is a priceless gift, the gift of knowing and loving another person, and of being known and of being loved. None of these gifts do we reject. But in meditation we stand back from all of them and, in that very process, we discover a harmony and an integration that become the basis of all our subsequent use of these great human gifts we have been given. The peace, the stillness and the harmony that we experience in meditation become the basis for all our action. . . .

When we meditate, not only do we stand back from the individual operations of our being, but we begin to learn to find a wholly new ground to stand on. We discover a rootedness of being which is not just in ourselves, because we discover ourselves rooted in God. Rooted in God who is Love.
John Main

Taking contemplation in the broad sense there is I think a great need to encourage the spirit of wonder at things as they are, the appreciation of and delight in beautiful things, sights and sounds, the concern for being as well as doing. This contemplative spirit is at variance with the get rich motive that supplies most of the drive behind the technological revolution but it is of vital importance for humanity. The Church ought not simply to adapt itself to the changing world but to witness to the primacy of the spiritual, of contemplation over action, of wisdom over ingenuity, of character over efficiency. Of course we want contemplation *and* action, ingenuity *and* wisdom, efficiency *and* character. But it makes a lot of difference which comes first.

Christopher Bryant

The Church of recent centuries, apart from the religious orders, has done little to encourage contemplation in the narrower sense of the experience and love of God. And for this reason it is finding it difficult to understand or channel into the Christian community the widespread interest among the young in yoga and other forms of eastern meditation. A church ought to be a place where those who wish to meditate could find the quiet and freedom from interruption that they need. I realize that churches are not in fact much used for this purpose, but in looking to the future we ought to bear this in mind.

Christopher Bryant

In essence, meditation is simply being still at the centre of your being. Being still.

John Main

When you look at a tree and see a tree, you have really not seen the tree. When you look at a tree and see a miracle – then, at last, you have seen a tree . . .
  That is the essence of Contemplation: the sense of Wonder. . . . This is the prerogative of the child. He is so often in a state of wonder. So he is naturally at home in the Kingdom of Heaven.

Anthony de Mello

Did you hear that bird sing?

Anthony de Mello

Do we slowly begin to observe that this God really is not any kind of particular being, a particular concrete Thou alongside every other thing that we know?
  Do we observe that we possess God, so to speak, only in silent adoration of the ineffable, sacred, incomprehensible mystery? . . . When we have seen all this and have the courage

to speak into this silence which seems to devour us the words 'Our Father', then only, I think, out of that which robs men today of their courage to pray, there really dawns upon us the true and final essence of prayer.

Karl Rahner

The way to the union of Christendom does not lie through committee-rooms, though there is a task of formulation to be done there. It lies through personal union with the Lord so deep and real as to be comparable with His union with the Father.

William Temple

Quiconque accède à la contemplation se change en semence. (Anyone who is admitted to contemplation is transformed into seed).

Antoine de St. Exupéry

> I give you the end of a golden string;
> Only wind it into a ball,
> It will lead you in at heaven's gate,
> Built in Jerusalem's wall.

William Blake

II
THE CHRIST

8

LOVE OF GOD FOR US

What fascinates me in God is his humility. God doesn't impose himself. God is neither a dictator nor an army commander. He never forces our hand. God is so careful of human freedom that at times he is so silent that our hearts almost break. God made himself humble so as not to blind us by his overwhelming, infinite beauty, by a love which would overpower us. God gives all and asks nothing in return. That is why, for anyone who chooses the absolute of his call, there is no happy medium. Being women and men of communion means always coming closer to an invisible martyrdom, it means bearing in our bodies the marks of Jesus Christ. And that means becoming a sign of God's radiance, a sign of resurrection, a sign of the absolute of his love. It means continually being able to turn our lives into a poem of love with God.

Roger Schutz

There are two kinds of love: one man loves whatever his clever son does and says, and boasts about his doing clever things and speaking clever words; the other loves his son for himself, no matter what he may say or do.

It is the same with the love of God for man. When a tried and proven man keeps the commandments and does good works wisely and well, God loves what he does and is present in all that he does, and thus the outer being of the universe is bound to God. But when the tried and proven man clings to God with his own being, then God loves him even when he does not work wisely and well, but goes his way with a simple mind and clings to God. God loves him just for that reason. And so the inner being of the universe is lifted to God.

Chasidic

The Love that moves the sun and the other stars.
Dante Alighieri

    Fear wist not to evade as Love wist to pursue.
       Still with unhurrying chase,
       And unperturbed pace,
Deliberate speed, majestic instancy,
       Came on the following Feet,
       And a Voice above their beat –
'Naught shelters thee, who wilt not shelter Me.'

       Now of that long pursuit
       Comes on at hand the bruit;
That Voice is round me like a bursting sea:
       'And is thy earth so marred,
       Shattered in shard on shard?
Lo, all things fly thee, for thou fliest Me!

All which I took from thee I did but take,
       Not for thy harms,
But just that thou might'st seek it in My arms.
       All which thy child's mistake
Fancies as lost, I have stored for thee at home:
       Rise, clasp My hand, and come!'

       Halts by me that footfall:
       Is my gloom, after all,
Shade of His hand, outstretched caressingly?
       'Ah, fondest, blindest, weakest,
       I am He Whom thou seekest!
Thou dravest love from thee, who dravest Me.'
Francis Thompson

Faith tends to be defeated by the burning presence of God in mystery, and seeks refuge from him, flying to comfortable social forms and safe conventions in which purification is no longer an inner battle but a matter of outward gesture.
Thomas Merton

There lives the dearest freshness deep down things;
And though the last lights from the black west went,
　Oh, morning at the brown brink eastwards springs –

　　　　Because the Holy Ghost over the bent

　　　　World broods with warm

　　　　　breast, and with,

　　　　　　ah, bright

　　　　　　　wings.

G.M. Hopkins

He prayeth well, who loveth well
Both man and bird and beast.
He prayeth best, who loveth best
All things both great and small;
For the dear God who loveth us,
He made and loveth all.

S.T. Coleridge

I heard by chance of the existence of those English poets of the seventeenth century who are named metaphysical. I discovered the poem . . . called 'Love'. I learnt it by heart. Often . . . I make myself say it over, concentrating all my attention upon it, and clinging with all my soul to the tenderness it enshrines. I used to think I was merely reciting it as a beautiful poem, but without my knowing it the recitation had the virtue of a prayer. It was during one of these recitations that, as I told you, Christ himself came down and took possession of me.

　Until last September I had never once prayed to God in all my life.

Simone Weil

Love bade me welcome; yet my soul drew back,
   Guilty of dust and sin
But quick-eyed Love, observing me grow slack
   From my first entrance in,
Drew nearer to me, sweetly questioning
   If I lack'd anything.

'A guest,' I answer'd, 'worthy to be here:'
   Love said, 'You shall be he,'
'I, the unkind, ungrateful? Ah, my dear,
   I cannot look on Thee.'
Love took my hand and smiling did reply,
   'Who made the eyes but I?'

'Truth, Lord, but I have marr'd them: let my shame
   Go where it doth deserve.'
'And know you not,' says Love. 'Who bore the blame?'
   'My dear, then I will serve.'
'You must sit down,' says Love, 'and taste my meat.'
   So I did sit and eat.

George Herbert

For God so loved the world that he gave his only Son, that whoever believes in him should not perish but have eternal life.

John 3:16

Where love and charity is, there is God.

Anon

Roger Schutz sees the love of God as his humility, – his refusal of any kind of coercion in his respect for human freedom. This is the answer to all those questions as to why God does not stop war, or concentration camps, or other atrocities. To prevent men from doing evil is to deny their freedom, their very humanity. It is the temptation of all human rulers whether in church or state. Few can resist it altogether.

   The Chasidic passage compares the love of God to that of a father who 'loves his son for himself, no matter what he may say or do.' Such parental love is rare; it is the essence of divine love.

   Francis Thompson sees the love of God as a relentless pursuit from which we flee for fear of what we may have to give up, or even for fear that we may lose our very self, if we allow ourselves to be caught. In the end there is no escape, yet what appeared to be lost is found to be infinite gain.

Hopkins sees God's love brooding over a world spoiled by 'man's smudge', and therein lies our ground of hope.

For Coleridge God's love calls us in response to love all His creation.

For Simone Weil and George Herbert God's love is expressed in His welcome for the unworthy guest.

All these are different ways of experiencing something far beyond our power to describe or communicate. Yet each in his or her own way has seen and experienced the same truth.

The Father, who is the source of everything in heaven and earth, loves and reveals; in him there is no clinging to power, no manipulation, no competition, and in this he is radically different from the *kosmos* he has created. His Son looks at him and reflects what he sees. Like the Father he lets go all power, and in this letting go he receives everything back. Here is the mystery of the to and fro of Love. As the Son lets go everything, he receives back from the Father the power of his authority and the light of his glory which transform the *kosmos* into the kingdom. And as the Father lets go that power and reveals that glory, he receives back from his Son the worship of a new world order.

Stephen Verney

The Power of God is the worship he inspires.

A.N. Whitehead

Whatever God does the first outburst is compassion.

Meister Eckhart

O Jerusalem, Jerusalem, . . . how often I have longed to gather your children together, as a hen gathers her chicks under her wings.

Matthew 23:37

9

LOVE TOWARDS GOD

Thou hast made us for thyself and our heart is restless till it find rest in Thee.

Augustine of Hippo

My spirit longeth for Thee
Within my troubled breast
Altho' I be unworthy
Of so divine a Guest.

Of so divine a Guest
Unworthy tho' I be,
Yet has my heart no rest
Unless it come from Thee.

Unless it come from Thee
In vain I look around:
In all that I can see,
No rest is to be found.

No rest is to be found,
But in Thy blessed Love;
O! let my wish be crown'd
And send it from above!

John Byrom

I always think that the best way to God is to love many things; that is what I say to myself. But one must love with a lofty and serious intimate sympathy, with strength, with intelligence: and one must try to know deeper and better and more. That leads to God . . .

Vincent Van Gogh

There is a well-known prayer which speaks of loving God 'above all things'. Van Gogh tells his brother Leo that the best way to God is to love many things. Perhaps the prayer should be amended to read 'loving Thee in and above all things'. Some of the sayings of Augustine suggest that to love God we have to abandon the love of things, yet elsewhere, as in the following quotation, he makes it clear that things are good and to be loved, but only where they lead to the love of God, as for Van Gogh, and do not distract us from him.

Those things are Yours, O God. They are good because you created them. None of our evil is in them. The evil is ours if we love them at the expense of Yourself – these things that reflect your design.

Augustine of Hippo

One cannot feel unmixed love for a mediocre moral standard any more than one can for the work of a mediocre artist.

Iris Murdoch

More! More! is the cry of a mistaken soul; less than All cannot satisfy Man.

William Blake

The moralists cease to be realistic and commit idolatry inasmuch as they worship, not God, but their own ethical ideals, inasmuch as they treat virtue as an end in itself and not as the necessary condition of the knowledge and love of God – a knowledge and love without which that virtue will never be made perfect or even socially effective.

Aldous Huxley

I wish you, then, a very rich, deep, true, straight and simple growth in the love of God, accepted and willed gently but greatly, at the daily, hourly cost of self.

Von Hügel

> In the deserts of the heart
> Let the healing fountain start,
> In the prison of his days
> Teach the free man how to praise.

W.H. Auden

Only in prison, brooding for years at a time, does he (Havel) eventually find occasional 'peace of mind', when 'all the pain of existence ceases to be paid and becomes what Christians call mercy'. A person will then readily accept a punishment, even if it has been meted out by the wrong authorities for a given offence – making that person a penitent – but to what authority? . . .

Does this make the penitent who is searching for an authority a 'God-seeker?'

This could well be someone who shrinks from saying the word 'God'; what we are possibly dealing with here is the manifestation of a new form of religiousness, which out of *courtesy* no longer addresses God with the name which has been trampled underfoot by politicians.

Heinrich Böll

Like as the hart desireth the water-brooks: so longeth my soul after thee, O God.

Psalm 42: 1a

God, of your goodness give me yourself for you are sufficient for me. I cannot properly ask anything less, to be worthy of you. If I were to ask less, I should always be in want. In you alone do I have all.

Julian of Norwich

Both Saint and Poet undergo a preparation for their work; and in both a notable feature of this preparation is a period of preliminary retirement . . .

In Poet as in Saint, this retirement is a process of pain and struggle. For it is nothing else than a gradual conformation to artistic law. He absorbs the law into himself; or rather he is himself absorbed into the law, moulded to it, until he becomes sensitively respondent to its faintest motion, as the spiritualised body to the soul. Thenceforth he needs no guidance from formal rule, having a more delicate rule within himself . . . In like manner does the Saint receive into himself and become one with divine law, whereafter he no longer needs to follow where the flocks have trodden, to keep the beaten track of rule; his will has undergone the heavenly magnetisation by which it points always and unalterably towards God.

Francis Thompson

'This is the covenant that I will make with the house of Israel after that time,' declares the Lord. 'I will put my law in their minds and write it on their hearts.'

Jeremiah 31: 33(a)

We love because he loved us first. But if a man says, 'I love God', while hating his brother, he is a liar. If he does not love the brother whom he has seen, it cannot be that he loves God whom he has not seen.

1 John 4:20

> My joy, my life, my crown!
>   My heart was meaning all the day,
>   Somewhat it fain would say:
> And still it runneth mutt'ring up and down
> With onely this, *My joy, my life, my crown.*

George Herbert

10

INCARNATION

Jesus Christ is the One in whom human selfhood fully came to its own and lived its fullest life, as human life ought to be lived, because His human selfhood was wholly yielded to God, so that His whole life was the life of God. That was the one life which was wholly divine and wholly human. He lived His life in such a way that it was the life of God incarnate; but also, since the initiative is always with God, He lived it as He did because it was the life of God incarnate. And thus through Him there came to those who knew Him a new revelation of God.

Donald Baillie

We saw that in the prophets the personal 'somewhat' which made them vehicles of truth could best be described by saying that God imparted to them something of Himself, thereby making them the men they were. This determined their attitude to experience. If now we discern in Jesus an attitude to experience which is unique in quality, we cannot but say that God imparted Himself to Jesus uniquely, and that the whole of what Jesus was expressed that self-impartation of God. This is formulated theologically in the doctrine of the Incarnation.

C.H. Dodd

This is the perspective which we have to recover if we are to understand the secret of monastic life. No matter how vast the space of the stellar universe may be, or how extensive the span of time we must allow for the evolution of the world, neither space nor time are of any significance in comparison with the fact that at a certain point in space and time the eternal, infinite Being, which we call God, was manifested in the span of a

human life. This is the supreme fact in comparison with which all human science and history pales into insignificance.
Dom Bede Griffiths

The meeting of myth and history in the Incarnation was the turning point in the history of religion . . . But it was not simply that myth had been fulfilled in history and was now outgrown, but rather that myth was revealed as a dimension of history and history as a dimension of myth.
Dom Bede Griffiths

The traditional term 'Incarnation' does little to suggest that in Christian experience God is known as activity or operation rather than as substance, or to facilitate the understanding of the life of Jesus as the point at which the divine Agape has embodied itself in human actions in the midst of earthly history.

To say that (the divine Agape has been inhistorised in the person of Jesus) is to say that the compassion and concern which were expressed in Jesus' dealings with men and women whom he met were identical with God's Agape towards those particular individuals.
John Hick

Our thinking today has, I am convinced, to begin 'from below' and move from immanence to transcendence, from relationships to revelation, from the Son of Man to the Son of God, rather than the other way round.
John A.T. Robinson

We are here reflecting upon an event that is beyond human understanding. All attempts to describe or explain it fall far short of the reality; therefore we do not assume that one attempt to throw light upon it necessarily excludes other quite different attempts to do so. That would be the kind of dogmatism which claims to possess the truth and in so doing hinders us from ever approaching it. As Edward Schillebeeckx has put it: 'being precise about an event that is a mystery always improverishes it'.

Jesus does not say 'Yes, I am equal to God', and he does not say, 'No, I am not equal to God.' With great accuracy and clarity he describes the relation between Father and Son, so that in the light of what he reveals to us the word 'equal' disappears.

Stephen Verney

All statements about divine sonship, pre-existence, creation mediatorship and incarnation – often clothed in the mythological and semi-mythological forms of the time – are meant in the last resort to do no more and no less than substantiate the uniqueness, underivability and unsurpassability of the call, offer and claim made known in and with Jesus, ultimately not of human but of divine origin and therefore absolutely reliable requiring mens' unconditional involvement.

Hans Küng

Commenting on John 10:32–39 R.E. Brown writes:

'Such a description of Jesus is not divorced from the fact that Jesus was sent by God and acted in God's name and in God's place. Therefore, although the Johannine description and acceptance of the divinity of Jesus has ontological implications . . ., in itself this description remains primarily functional and not too far removed from the Pauline formulation that 'God was in Christ reconciling the world to himself'.

(2 Corinthians 5:19)

Jesus' being as man is 'God translated' for us.

Edward Schillebeeckx

The religious value of the doctrine of the Incarnation is not found in what it affirms concerning the historical figure, Jesus of Nazareth, but in what it affirms concerning the eternal God. When we know that all the grace and truth which shine in Jesus Christ are shining through Him from the Father, we begin to understand who and what God really is.

William Temple

Our 'worldly' language may be that of poetry, or politics, or personal relationships. Yet, whether specific 'God'-talk is a help or a hindrance, it is 'transcendence *within* immanence' that we have somehow to articulate and express.

John A.T. Robinson

God is Christlike and in him is no unChristlikeness at all.
Michael Ramsey

I never asked myself whether Jesus was, or was not, an incarnation of God, but simply as a matter of fact I found myself incapable of thinking about him without thinking about him as God.
Simone Weil

We saw his glory, such glory as befits the Father's only Son, full of grace and truth.
John 1:14

11

THE CHRIST

What, then, does Jesus mean to me? To me, He was one of the greatest teachers humanity has ever had. To his believers, He was God's only begotten son. Could the fact that I do not accept this belief make Jesus have any more or less influence in my life? . . . I cannot believe so . . . My interpretation . . . is that in Jesus's own life is the key to his nearness to God; that he expressed, as no other could, the spirit and will of God. It is in this sense that I see Him and recognise Him as the son of God.
M.K. Gandhi

If Jesus presented Himself as one in whose life God was active, He did so not primarily by the use of titles, or by clear statements about what He was, but rather by the impact of His person and His life on those who followed Him.
Raymond Brown

To the Greek the Messiah was as strange a thought as to ourselves. To us the Logos is as strange as the Messiah was to the Greek. We have really at present no terms in which to express what we feel to be the permanent significance of Jesus, and the old expressions may repel us until we realize, first, that they are not of the original essence of the Gospel, and second, that they represent the best language which Greek or Jew could find for a conviction which we share – that Jesus of Nazareth does stand in the centre of human history, that he has brought God and man into a new relation, that he is the personal concern of every one of us, and that there is more in him that we have yet accounted for.
T.R. Glover

The word 'Christ' is the Greek translation of the Hebrew 'Messiah' meaning 'the anointed one'. In this sense every Jewish king was a 'Christ' – anointed as a king by divine right. The word itself does not imply divinity, though it clearly does imply divine appointment. There is much difference of opinion as to whether Jesus claimed to be the Messiah: what does seem clear is that, if he accepted or claimed the title, he certainly re-interpreted it. His rebuke to Peter (Mark 8:33) and the so-called triumphal entry into Jerusalem (an acting out of the prophesy of Zechariah 9:9) show that he rejected the role of a national leader against the Romans; rather it was 'to fight abuse at the heart of Judaism' (C.F.D. Moule) and to proclaim, in word and action, a Messiah in continuity with the best in the prophetic tradition, and in radical discontinuity with the priestly tradition. The prophetic tradition included the Suffering Servant of Isaiah 53, the forgiving God of Hosea, the 'option for the poor' of Amos, the gentle king of Zechariah. It is not difficult to see Jesus (as he probably saw himself) as the fulfilment of that tradition.

If we say with Paul that 'God was in Christ reconciling the world to himself' we mean that in Christ the divine Agape was at work dealing with sinful humanity. And if we say, as twentieth-century theologians, that in the life of Jesus christian faith finds, not divine substance injected into a human frame, but divine action taking place in and through a human life, we mean that in that life is uniquely to be seen the divine Agape directly at work within our human sphere.

John Hick

Truly man: Against all tendencies to deify Jesus, it must constantly be stressed even to-day that he was wholly and entirely man with all the consequences of this (capacity for suffering, fear, loneliness, insecurity, temptations, doubts, possibility of error). Not merely man, but true man. In describing him as such we insisted on the truth which has to be made true, the unity of theory and practice, of acknowledging and following him, of faith and action. As true man, by his proclamation, behavior and fate, he was a model of what it is to be human, enabling each and everyone who commits himself to him to discover and to realize the meaning of being man and of his freedom to exist for his fellow men. As confirmed by God, he therefore represents the permanently reliable ultimate standard of human existence.

Hans Küng

What was the true nature of Christ's words. Were they the beginning of an era of salvation and one of the most powerful cultural impulses in the history of the world – or were they the spiritual source of the crusades, inquisitions, the cultural extermination of the Americas, and later, the entire expansion of the white race that was fraught with so many contradictions and had so many tragic consequences, including the fact that most of the human world had been consigned to that wretched category known as the 'third' world?

I still tend to think that His words belonged to the former category, but at the same time I cannot ignore the umpteen books that demonstrate that even in its purest and earliest form there was something unconsciously encoded in Christianity which, when combined with a thousand and one other circumstances, including the relative permanence of human nature, could in some way pave the way spiritually even for the sort of horrors I mentioned.

Vaclav Havel

Havel speaks of something 'unconsciously encoded in Christianity' which led to the horrors to which he refers. Does he mean to distinguish Christianity from Christ? Did the horrors spring from something unconsciously encoded in Christ's teaching or from the post-Constantinian Church and its dangerous compromise with the State? The Grand Inquisitor (see page 220) thought they sprang from Christ himself. Many Christians take the other view.

He (Jesus) is . . . from many different starting-points, the one who opens up the way to God – as they variously conceived that way to be.

J. L. Houlden

Something in the world had been changed – Rome was at an end. The reign of numbers was at an end. The duty, imposed by armed force to live unanimously as a people, as a whole nation, was abolished. Leaders and nations belonged to the past. They were replaced by the doctrine of personality and

freedom. The story of a human life became the life story of God and filled the universe. As it says in the liturgy for the Feast of the Annunciation, Adam tried to be a God and failed, but now God was made man so that Adam should be made God.
Boris Pasternak

> With this ambiguous earth
> His dealings have been told us. These abide:
> The signal to a maid, the human birth,
> The lesson, and the young Man crucified.
>
> But not a star of all
> The innummerable host of stars has heard
> How he administered this terrestrial ball.
> Our race have kept their Lord's entrusted Word.
>
> O be prepared, my soul!
> To read the inconceivable, to scan
> The million forms of God those stars unroll
> When, in our turn, we show to them a Man.
>
> *Alice Meynell*

And to anticipate by taking an illustration from the realm of unconditional relation: how powerful, even to being overpowering, and how legitimate, even to being self-evident, is the saying of I by Jesus. For it is the I of unconditional relation in which the man calls his Thou Father in such a way that he himself is simply Son, and nothing else but Son.
Martin Buber

For John, Jesus is not God *simpliciter*, Jesus is a man who incarnates in everything he is and does the Logos who is God. He is the Son, the mirror image of God, who is God for man and in man. The 'I' of Jesus speaks God, acts God. He utters the things of God, he does the works of God. He is his plenipotentiary, totally commissioned to represent him – as a human being.
John A.T. Robinson

The categories in which people have recently attempted to convey the meaning of Christ have been those such as the servant-Lord, the way, the man for others, the victim, the outsider, the representative, the incognito, even the clown or harlequin, whose pathos and weakness and irony, as well as whose gaiety and freedom, 'all begin to make a strange kind of sense again'. Yet *in* all these he is to be seen as the embodiment of 'the beyond' – in our midst.

John A.T. Robinson

Jesus might be unique in his place in the history of Israel and in the role he has since played in the growth of the churches, in the religious history of the world. Thus there arise 'functional christologies', which make the human life of Jesus a focal point of historical divine interaction with humanity, rather than saying that Jesus is the same being as God.

Keith Ward

'Tis the weakness in strength that I cry for!
My flesh that I seek.
In the Godhead! I seek and I find it. O Saul, it shall be
A Face like my face that receives thee; a Man like to me,
Thou shalt love and be loved by, for ever: a Hand like this hand
Shall throw open the gates of new life to thee' See the Christ
   stand!'

Robert Browning

12

DEATH

No dying figure in Shakespeare looks forward; they all look backward; none thirst for the otherness of God, they all enjoy, or suffer in, and with, and for, the visible, or at least the immanent alone.

Von Hügel

To be ready (for death) has never seemed to mean anything to me but this: to be straining forwards.

Teilhard de Chardin

To receive communion as I die is not sufficient: teach me to make a communion of death itself.

Teilhard de Chardin

The great triumph of the Creator and Redeemer, from a Christian viewpoint, is to have transformed into an essential life-giving factor that which in itself is a universal life-diminishing force leading to extinction. In order to penetrate us definitively God must in some way make a void within us, empty us, so as to make room for himself. In order to unite us to himself, he must reshape us, recast us, break up the very molecules of our being. It is the role of death to bring about the desired opening up of the deepest level of our personality.

Teilhard de Chardin

Here we are challenged to a positive view of death. For most of us old age or serious illness is a decline into death. Teilhard de Chardin challenges us to look forward to death as a positive goal. In old age our very 'diminutions' provide an opportunity to centre our lives in God in a way that is far more difficult, if not impossible, in a busy life occupied with many things. Death opens up to God as nothing else can the deepest level of our personality. This does not necessarily mean that we can face death with equanimity – Jesus did not, Dylan Thomas suggests that we should not – but, as Hans Küng declares in the following quotation, 'This fear and this trembling (may we add 'and this rage'?) are encompassed by God who is love'.

Love is, of course, and remains the triumph over death, but that is not because it abolishes death, but because it is itself death. Only in death is the total surrender that is love's possible, for only in death can we be exposed completely and without reserve.

Ladislaus Boros

> Do not go gentle into that good night,
> Old age should turn and rave at close of day;
> Rage, rage against the dying of the light.

Dylan Thomas

When it comes to dying, the Christian must not behave like the stoic, must not suppress emotions, deny passions, put on an act of emotional coolness and composure. Jesus Christ did not die like a stoic in dispassionate serenity, as painlessly as possible, but in great torment with the cry of one forsaken by God. In the face of this death the Christian need not deny his fear and trembling but, – with Jesus's fear of death behind him, Jesus's cry still in his ears – he may be certain too that this fear and this trembling are encompassed by God who is love, are transformed into the freedom of the children of God.

Hans Küng

One wears his mind out in study, and yet has more mind with which to study. One gives away his heart in love and yet has more heart to give away. One perishes out of pity for a suffering world, and is the stronger therefor. So, too, it is possible at one and the same time to hold on to life and let it go.

Milton Steinberg

When death, the great Reconciler, has come, it is never our tenderness that we repent of, but our severity.

George Eliot

When Jesus speaks of the dead, he uses the word in two senses. On the physical level the dead are the corpses which we bury in tombs, but on the level of Spirit they are those who may appear to be alive in an earthly sense, but who inwardly are dead. They have never come alive, because they do not know the truth of God springing up within themselves. Jesus brought these two senses together when he said, 'Let the dead bury their dead' – for at a funeral it is not only the corpse in the coffin who may be dead, but also the mourners and the officiating minister.
Stephen Verney

Poor soul, the centre of my sinful earth,
Fool'd by these rebel powers that thee array,
Why dost thou pine within and suffer dearth,
Painting thy outward walls so costly gay?
Why so large cost, having so short a lease,
Dost thou upon thy fading mansion spend?
Shall worms, inheritors of this excess,
Eat up thy charge? Is this thy body's end?
Then, soul, live thou upon thy servant's loss,
And let that pine to aggravate thy store;
Buy terms divine in selling hours of dross;
Within be fed, without be rich, no more:
   So shalt thou feed on Death, that feeds on men,
   And Death once dead, there's no more dying then.
William Shakespeare

No crystal palace of this life, no just order of society, gives any guarantee for humanity. The one thing that matters is the belief in the transcendence of human life – let us speak plainly as Dostoyevsky himself does: the one thing is whether or not there is belief in immortality.
Rauschning

We shall die alone.
Blaise Pascal

    I have a sin of feare, that when I have spunne
    My last thread, I shall perish on the shore,
    Sweare by thy selfe, that at my death thy sonne

> Shall shine as he shines now, and heretofore;
> And, having done that, Thou hast done,
>   I feare no more.
>
> *John Donne*

Positively, this Night, that Star so very bright over the mast of a noble Vessel – & the sound of the water breaking against the Ship Side – it seems quite a *Home* to me . . . Death *itself* will be only a Voyage – a Voyage not *from*, but to our native Country.

S.T. Coleridge

In the last analysis it is our conception of death which decides our answers to the questions life puts to us.

Dag Hammarskjold

> Here in the body pent
> Absent from Him I roam,
> Yet Nightly pitch my moving tent
> A day's march nearer home.
>
> *James Montgomery*

A visitor was trying to comfort a dying man in hospital. The patient asked for some assurance about future life. Suddenly there was a scratching at the door of the patient's room. 'Do you hear that noise?' said the visitor, 'that is my dog: I left him downstairs. He has no idea what is on this side of the door but he heard his master's voice and knows his master is here.'

Father, into thy hands I commit my spirit.

Luke 23:46

13

RESURRECTION

Resurrection means dying into God.
 Dying into God is not something to be taken for granted, not a natural development . . . Death is man's affair, resurrection can only be God's. Man is taken up, called, brought home, and therefore finally accepted, saved, by God into himself as the incomprehensible, comprehensive ultimate reality.

Hans Küng

The Gospel as it was first proclaimed, the Gospel which converted the Roman Empire and reclaimed our fierce pagan ancestors for Christian civilisation and ordered liberty, was not extracts from the Sermon on the Mount. It was far more tragic and far more realistic. It was the story of a Young Man, dedicated to a new age of Love and Truth, Righteousness and Freedom, murdered by a totalitarian state, in uttermost agony of mind and body, broken by the hard facts of life, His claim discredited and His cause lost, who held on through disaster and defeat serene in His confidence in God, and in the hour of failure was victorious.

F.R. Barry

The claims of earliest Christianity were based not, primarily at least, on claims explicitly made by Jesus, but rather on the implications of his life, his actions, his teaching, his death, and, most notably, its extraordinary sequel.

C.F.D. Moule

The resurrection is not the legitimation or verification of this (prophetic) message, nor the basis of Christian faith: we do not

legitimate a point of faith, viz. faith in the message of Jesus, with another point of faith, our belief in this resurrection. Despite Jesus' death, Christian faith is a matter of belief in his prophetic message and promise.
Edward Schillebeeckx

Trusting God, living in faith and love, include accepting the fact that we cannot see how it can be – it certainly looks as if we altogether die – but we believe that trusting and loving are raised to continue on another shore and in a greater light. This belief is not arrived at by any inference from events in this world. It is to be traced to the fact that trusting and loving simply add up to that kind of serene expectation.
Neville Ward

A Professor of Mathematical Physics (John Polkinghorne) spoke about the way almost all the atoms in our body change every seven years, yet the pattern they form persists. Although the material which constitutes our body has changed we are still recognisably the same person. So, he believed, although there is no material identity between our body in this life and the next, yet it is possible to imagine the same pattern (i.e. identity of personality) being recreated in some other world.

We believe that the risen Christ has continuity of personal identity with Jesus of Nazareth, however 'exalted' or 'glorified' (to use the New Testament terms) the risen Christ may be; we believe it to be true about those in Christ who will be raised up at the last day; we believe that, however changed, they will be recognizably themselves: the pattern of their personality will be recreated.

There is in sickness a grace which brings us near to realities which lie beyond death.
Antoine de St. Exupéry

Just as

a person

casts off

worn-out garments

and puts on

others

that are new,

even so does the embodied-soul cast off worn-out bodies and takes on others that are new.

Bhagavadgita 2:22

The fact that God intervenes at the point where everything is at an end from the human point of view, this – despite the maintenance of natural laws – is the true miracle of the resurrection: the miracle of the beginning of a new life out of death. It is not an object of historical knowledge, but certainly a call and an offer to faith, which alone can get at the reality of the person raised up.

Hans Küng

While for the first year of my imprisonment I did nothing else, and can remember doing nothing else, but wring my hands in impotent despair, and say, 'What an ending, what an appalling ending', now I try to say to myself, and sometimes when I am not torturing myself do really and sincerely say, 'What a beginning, what a wonderful beginning'.

Oscar Wilde

At first the resurrection is presented to us as an event outside of ourselves, something which happened two thousand years ago. Slowly, if our faith is developing, we come to know the resurrection as something which is happening to us now. The risen Christ is continuously coming through the closed doors of our minds and imagination as he came through the doors of the room where the disciples were gathered for fear of the Jews. He enters our consciousness, closed through fear of ourselves and our fear of other people, and says to us, 'Peace be to you'. The power of his resurrection gives us hope in a situation where before we felt it was hopeless, gives us courage to face a task when before we wanted to run away, gives us the ability and strength to be open and vulnerable when before we could think of nothing but our own protection and security.

Gerard W. Hughes

There is a history of resurrections, which has vicarious significance. A person's resurrection is no personal privilege for himself alone – even if he is called Jesus of Nazareth. It contains within itself hope for all, for everything.

Dorothy Soelle

If we are ready for life in the sense of being open to its power and possibilities, then we are also ready for death. If we are aware of resurrection in the present, then we shall not be over-concerned about resurrection in the future. What Jesus said about becoming as little children and taking no thought for the morrow applies with special force to our future in and beyond the grave. We live now from hour to hour, from minute to minute, as those who are ever receiving from the unknown, and that is all we need to know.

H. A. Williams

> It might suit a number of the lords
> if death fixed everything for ever
> confirmed eternally
> the lordship of the lords
> the Servitude of the Servants.

It might suit a number of the lords
to remain lords for ever
in their costly private tombs
their servants still serving
in row on row of cheap graves

But there is a resurrection
different from what we thought
resurrection that is
God's revolt against the lords
and against the lord of lords: death.
Kurt Marti

We must be still and still moving
Into another intensity
For a further vision, a deeper
   communion.
T. S. Eliot

14

SALVATION/NEWNESS OF LIFE

Batter my heart, three person'd God; for you
As yet but knocke, breathe, shine and seek to mend:
That I may rise, and stand, o'erthrow me, and bend
Your force, to breake, blowe, burn and make me new.
John Donne

Redemption or salvation ... is essentially restoration to wholeness, i.e. it concerns man in the totality of his worldly existence. In contrast to the older, though not the New Testament, view that salvation is *from* something, e.g. from the world, from hell etc., we now have a positive understanding that it comprises the achievement of a full life now.
J.G. Davis

Destructiveness is the outcome of unlived life.
Erich Fromm

One sure test of right living and right dispositions is the degree to which such living and dispositions make zest to prevail in our lives and make excitement to disappear from them.
Von Hügel

Zest is the pleasure which comes from thoughts, occupation, etc., that fit into, that are continuous, applications, etc., of extant habits and interests of a good kind – duties and joys that steady us and give us balance and centrality. Excitement is the pleasure which comes from breaking loose, from fragmentariness, from losing our balance and centrality. Zest is natural warmth – excitement is fever heat. For zest – to be relished – requires much self-discipline and recollection – much spaciousness of mind: whereas the more distracted we are, the more racketed and impulse-led, the more we thirst for excitement and the more its sirocco air dries up our spiritual sap and makes us long for more excitement . . .

Von Hügel

During the past thirty years people from all the civilized countries of the earth have consulted me . . . Among all my patients in the second half of life – that is to say over thirty-five – there has not been one whose problem in the last resort was not that of finding a religious outlook on life. It is safe to say that every one of them fell ill because he had lost that which the living religions of every age have given to their followers, and none of them has been really healed who did not regain that religious outlook.

C.G. Jung

The message of the Gospel is that God has begun in Jesus Christ a new divine order of life, of which Christ is the centre and the head. By His saving Will He commences the restoration of the original and normal divine life-order, in which the worship of God and the joyful doing of His will are the *natural* life.

This restoration took in Christ its beginning. His coming in the flesh marks the inauguration of the first term in God's work of redemption and reclaiming. The joyful doing of the holy will of God is not yet our natural life. We have understood through Christ that it ought to be so, but the powers of sin and confusion contend in us against it as long as this world stands. The integral realization of this new order, of the Kingdom of God, is the object of expectation . . . In the radical religious realism of the Bible this expectation is a real longing.

Hendrik Kraemer

Salvation cannot be identified exclusively with political liberation; exclusively with 'being nice to one another'; exclusively with ecological efforts; exclusively with identifying oneself either with micro-ethics or macro-ethics or with mysticism, liturgy and prayer; exclusively with concerning oneself with education or geriatric techniques, and so on. *All this* is part of the concept of the salvation or wholeness of mankind, and is therefore also essentially concerned with salvation from God, which may be experienced as grace.
Edward Schillebeeckx

The need for a reward, for receiving the equivalent of what we give. But if, in doing violence to that need, we leave a void, it produces something like an inrush of air, and a supernatural reward supervenes. It does not come if we receive any other payment: that void causes it to come.
Simone Weil

The entire ministry of Jesus during the period of his public life was not an assurance or promise of salvation but a concrete tender of salvation then and there. He does not just talk about God and his rule; where he appears he brings salvation and becomes God's rule already realised.

Jesus' Abba experience is an immediate awareness of God as a power cherishing people and making them free . . . Thus there is positive hope for everyone without exception.
Edward Schillebeeckx

The mark of the unredeemed man is the craving for things to compensate him for not being fully what he is.
H.A. Williams

It was only when St. Paul gave up trying to keep the law and instead saw and received what was offered to him that he found salvation. And he described this salvation as a new creation, the raising up of a new being, not as the overhaul and repair of the old one by frantic effort.
H.A. Williams

If the body is dead because it has been cut off from the rest of what we are, then it cannot be raised from the dead like an inanimate object which is lifted up or pushed around. What it needs is to have its own life given to it so that it can raise itself by its own inherent vitality. And this can happen only when the dualism between mind and body has been transcended. It is something we can neither think nor act ourselves into. There is no escaping the necessity of miracle.

H.A. Williams

On the (tennis) court, at least when I'm on form, I don't seem to be mind and body. I seem to be simply me. I suppose that is why the game is satisfying. While it lasts, I am not a man divided. Everything I am – mind and body – energizes as an organic whole, and I am not aware of divisions and distinctions within myself. But that, as I said, is when I am on form . . . When I'm off-form, my experience on the court is invariably the same. It is as if I am an inner mental man who is trying to use his body as a machine almost external to himself. It is no longer a case of mind and body being in such perfect rapport that they are indistinguishable . . . When I play a game well, I have for that limited period of time an experience of the body's resurrection . . . The resurrection of the body is both the resurrection of the flesh and of the entire man.

H.A. Williams

From hence it manifestly appears, what is the nature of the New Birth. It is that great change which God works in the soul, when he brings it into life; – when the love of the world is changed into the love of God; pride into humility; passion into meekness: hatred, envy, malice, into a sincere, tender, disinterested love for all mankind. In a word, it is that change whereby the earthly, sensual, devilish mind is turned into the 'mind which was in Christ Jesus'.

John Wesley

Somehow we should learn to know that our problems are our most precious possessions. They are the raw materials of our salvation: no problem – no redemption. And it is only by bringing to our problems the whole of ourselves – which means all that we have rejected in these specialized aspects of ourselves we call civilization – that life can be renewed in a greater dimension of itself. But these in-between moments are frightening; and they are the moments that the first people of Africa, who feared them most, attributed to 'a loss of soul'.

Laurens van der Post

A new creation? Only the God who created the universe can re-create a human being, but even he will not do this without our willing co- operation; any coercion would deny his original purpose in the creation of humankind.

The phrase 'born again Christian' is sometimes used very lightly. John Wesley's description of the New Birth should make us pause before speaking lightly or complacently of the radical change he describes.

In questioning our need for a recompense Simone Weil adds a further dimension of radical change, without which we cannot leave ourselves open to the Spirit.

All this was a long time ago, I remember
And I would do it again, but set down
This set down
This: were we led all that way for
Birth or Death? There was a Birth, certainly,
We had evidence and no doubt. I had seen birth and death
But had thought they were different; this Birth was
Hard and bitter agony for us, like Death, our death.
We returned to our palaces, these Kingdoms,
But no longer at ease here, in the old dispensation,
With an alien people clutching their gods.
I should be glad of another death.

T.S. Eliot

I don't know who – or what – put the question, I don't know when it was put. I don't even remember answering. But at some moment I did answer Yes to Someone – or Something – and from that hour I was certain that existence is meaningful and that, therefore, my life in self-surrender, had a goal. From that moment I have known what it means 'not to look back', and 'to take no thought for the morrow'.

Dag Hammarskjold

Hardness of heart and mercy:

The fourth vision gathered like a cloud of thick smoke and took on human form, but without arms or legs – only huge black eyes that stared unblinking. Perfectly still, it remained out there in the dark, motionless. It spoke:

HARDNESS OF HEART: I have produced nothing and brought no one into existence. So why should I bother about anything? I intend to leave things as they are and only help people when they are useful to me. God created everything; let him take care of it all! If I become involved, even just a little, in other people's affairs, what use would it do me? And even if I did, I would do them neither good nor harm. I could go around feeling pity for everyone and everything, but I wouldn't get a moment's peace; and what would become of me? What kind of life would I lead if I had to find an answer for every voice of joy or sadness? I know only that I myself exist; and everyone else should do the same.

Again I heard a voice from the cloud. It spoke:

MERCY'S REPLY: What are you saying, you creature of stone? The plants give off the fragrance of their flowers. The precious stones reflect their brilliance to others. Every creature yearns for a loving embrace. The whole of nature serves humanity, and in this service offers all her bounty. But you have not even merited full human form. All you are is a pitiless stare, an evil cloud of smoke in the darkness!
  But I am soothing herb. I dwell in the dew and in the air and in all greenness. My heart fills to overflowing and I give help to others. I was there when the first words resounded: 'Let there be'. From these words the whole of creation issued forth which stands today at the disposal of humanity. But you are excluded. With a loving eye, I observe the demands of life and feel myself a part of all. I lift up the broken-hearted and lead them to wholeness, since I am the balm for every pain, and since my words ring true while you remain what you are: a bitter cloud of smoke!

Hildegard of Bingen

The fundamental miracle: the transformation of human nature, with all its potential for evil, into 'the mind of Christ', with all its potential for good.

III
MEANS OF GRACE

15

BEAUTY

Heroism, ecstasy, prayer, love, surround a forehead with a halo because they free the soul, which makes its envelope transparent and sheds light all around it. Beauty is then a phenomenon of the spiritualisation of matter. Just as a powerful electric current can make metals luminous and reveal their essential nature by the colour of the flame, so fullness of life and the highest joy may render a simple mortal dazzlingly beautiful.

Henri Frederic Amiel

Oh, beautiful is love and to be free
Is beautiful, and beautiful are friends
Love, freedom, Comrades, surely make amends
For all these thorns through which we walk to death
God let us breathe your beauty with our breath.

James Elroy Flecker

Beauty, Good, and Knowledge are three sisters
And never can be sundered without tears

Anon

Now all the heavenly splendour
Breaks forth in starlight tender
From myriad worlds unknown.
   And man the marvel seeing,
   Forgets his selfish being,
For joy of beauty not his own.

*Robert Bridges
based on Paulus Gerhardt*

Almost all art is a form of fantasy-consolation and few artists achieve the vision of the real. The talent of the artist can be readily, and is naturally, employed to produce a picture whose purpose is the consolation and aggrandizement of its author and the projection of his personal obsessions and wishes. To silence and expel self, to contemplate and delineate nature with a clear eye, is not easy and demands a moral discipline. A great artist is, in respect of his work, a good man, and, in the true sense, a free man. The consumer of art has an analogous task to its producer: to be disciplined enough to see as much reality in the work as the artist has succeeded in putting into it, and not to 'use it as magic'. The appreciation of beauty in art or nature is not only (for all its difficulties) the easiest available spiritual exercise; it is also a completely adequate entry into (and not just analogy of) the good life, since it is the checking of selfishness in the interest of seeing the real.

Consider what we learn from contemplating the characters of Shakespeare or Tolstoy or the paintings of Velasquez or Titian. What is learnt here is something about the real quality of human nature, when it is envisaged, in the artist's just and compassionate vision, with a clarity which does not belong to the self-centred rush of ordinary life.

Iris Murdoch

The impulse to surrender, (George Eliot) suggests, so destructive when turned inwards, is closely akin to the artist's abnegation of self. But the latter is positive because it is turned outwards, into communication with others. In 'Daniel Deronda' shortly before he rescues Mirah, Daniel himself is drifting on the Thames:

'He chose a spot in the bend of the river just opposite Kew Gardens, where he had a great breadth of water before him reflecting the glory of the sky, while he himself was in shadow. He lay with his hands behind his head propped on a level with the boat's edge, so that he could see all around him, but could not be seen by anyone at a few yards distance: and for a long while he never turned his eyes from the view right in front of him. He was forgetting everything else in a half-speculative, half-involuntary identification of himself with the objects he was looking at, thinking how far it might be possible habitually to shift his centre till his own personality would be no less outside him than the landscape.'

George Eliot

The passage makes it clear that there is a way in which mortals can escape the bounds of self. Daniel's receptivity is extremely close both to what Keats described as the negative capability of the artist's imagination and to what George Eliot in all her earlier novels described as the essentially 'feminine' capacity to suppress the self in a relationship with another.

On a more direct level (George Eliot) presents art, and particularly music. as the one human activity which can transcend the boundaries of space and time. But there is a problem in raising culture to the level of salvation in this way. For Eliot is really writing only about a refined tradition of art, literature and music – Sophocles, Dante, Mozart – which is not accessible to those common people she set out at the start of her career to celebrate in her work. And even in elite circles the consolation of art is not open to all. For she insists that artistic talent, at the highest level, is a gift – backed up by training and hard work to be sure – but ultimately a quality of soul.

Jennifer Uglow

When Pasternak speaks of art as 'a possession', and the artist as one who is 'stricken, possessed by reality', what undoubtedly he has in mind is this capacity in us all to be taken over by reality, to be released, if only for a moment, from the ego-bound world by which we are most of the time possessed. It is thus not only the artist and the poet who are capable of this freedom; we are all able, being endowed with this faculty of imagination, to some extent to create, and continually to recreate, the world in which we live.

Edward Robinson

If it is . . . true that the artistic vision is deeper and more powerful than that of Philosophy, why may not religious thought in the future make the same kind of alliance with art as it has hitherto had with Philosophy? Why should not religion become spontaneously plural and creative?

Don Cupitt

Artists do not have the reputation of being unselfish, saintly people. This may be partly because their passion for their art is little understood by those around them; partly because they are people of heightened sensitivity who feel deeply and react impulsively. Yet, as Iris Murdoch maintains, the artist is, in respect of his work, a good man and, in the true sense, a free man. To contemplate nature with a clear eye involves a silencing of self which demands a moral discipline. Similarly she sees the appreciation of beauty in art or nature as a spiritual exercise, an entry into the good life. How far does this correspond with contemplation as a religious exercise?

In the prayerbook we use in my synagogue there is the story of a king who had a very large, beautiful diamond, but it had a flaw, a deep scratch down one side. He offered his daughter's hand in marriage to anyone who could erase it. Many tried – unsuccessfully. At length a gifted jeweller offered to make the rare diamond even more beautiful than it had been before the mishap. He kept his word. Instead of trying to erase the scratch, he used it as a stem upon which he engraved a rose. Then the flaw became a thing of beauty.

Rabbi Hugo Gryn

All art loses meaning and becomes merely repetitive when it loses contact with its religious motivation.

Wolfgang von Goethe

The purpose of art is to disturb; knowledge comforts us.

Georges Braque

Beauty, the creation of which has classically been regarded as the purpose of art, is too often defined in terms of what produces these feelings of comfort; of what relaxes tension, not of what creates it. The result is an enervated spirituality; the cause is an art reduced to imitation.

Edward Robinson

Prettiness does not demand arduousness but beauty does.

Matthew Fox

For many people nowadays music *is* a kind of religion. The ritual of the concert hall, the sense of occasion and togetherness, the emotional release, the hints of transcendence, the awareness of meaning which lies too deep for words – all these add up to a kind of religious experience which has the added advantage for many that it doesn't involve explicit meaning, needs, affirmations or obligations. Religion doesn't have to be all the time conscious, and wordy, and morally demanding.

But it does have to be sometimes, or it loses its roots in reality. And that is why occasions when marvellous music is linked through words to an incomparable action in the eucharist are so valuable. For those of us who begin, as it were, with the words, music can open up their depths. For those who begin with the music, the words can anchor ecstasy in the truly divine. Together they can bring us to the threshold between time and eternity.

John Habgood

> Blessed Cecilia, appear in visions
> To all musicians, appear and inspire:
> Translated Daughter, come down and startle
> Composing mortals with immortal fire.
>
> *W.H. Auden*

> We are the music makers,
> And we are the dreamers of dreams . . .
> Yet we are the movers and shakers
> Of the world forever it seems.
>
> *Arthur William Edgar O'Shaughnessy*

All other forms of art pale into insignificance compared with the art of Christ. We paint on canvas but Christ was an artist in flesh and blood.

Vincent van Gogh

We are heirs of the fearful creative power of God.

Meister Eckhart

16

TRUTH

You will know the truth, and the truth will make you free.
John 8:32

But when the Counselor comes, whom I shall send to you from the Father, even the Spirit of truth, who proceeds from the Father, he will bear witness to me.
John 15:26

The Church believes it has been promised God's presence in the form of guidance into the truth. The truth that is meant is not every kind of truth, the truth of the physical sciences for example, but the truth about God and his purpose in the world and what he wants done in particular situations.
Neville Ward

It seemed clear to me, and I still believe it to-day, that one can never offer too much resistance to God if one does it for the pure love of truth. Christ wants us to put truth first, even before himself, for before being the Christ he is the truth. If we turn away from him to go towards the truth we shall not go far before we fall into his arms.
Simone Weil

What sense does it make to speak of offering resistance to God or turning away from Christ 'for the pure love of truth'. There are those who claim that a world in which there is so much suffering, and especially the suffering of innocent children (see section entitled 'Suffering') cannot be reconciled with belief in a Creator God of love; there are those who believe that Christ's teaching of unconditional forgiveness undermines the moral law; those who believe that the teaching about loving our enemies, if taken seriously, would tend to upset the balance of power upon which, they believe, peace depends; those who identify Jesus with the persecuting church and therefore reject him. All these may be turning away from God or Christ 'for the pure love of truth'. They may be mistaken, but there is no reason to doubt their sincerity.

The commandment of absolute truthfulness is really only another name for the fullness of discipleship.

Dietrich Bonhoeffer

He who begins by loving Christianity better than Truth will proceed by loving his own sect or church better than Christianity, and end by loving himself better than all.

Samuel Taylor Coleridge

The need for truth is more sacred than any other. It is however never mentioned... there are men who work eight hours a day and make a big effort to read in the evening to educate themselves. They cannot find time to verify in the big libraries what they read. They believe what they read. We do not have the right to misinform them. What sense does it make to say that the authors wrote it in good faith? They do not work physically eight hours a day. Society feeds them so that they have the time and may take the trouble to avoid error.

A pointsman who caused a derailment would not be well received if he made the excuse that he did it in good faith. It is even more shameful to tolerate the existence of newspapers in which everyone knows that no contributor could stay unless he agreed at times consciously to detract from the truth.

There is no possibility of satisfying the need for truth in any nation if one cannot find for that purpose men who love the truth.

Simone Weil

Why was Solzhenitsyn driven out of his own country? Certainly not because he represented a unit of real power, that is, not because any of the regime's representatives felt he might unseat them and take their place in government. Solzhenitsyn's expulsion was something else: a desperate attempt to plug up the dreadful wellspring of truth, a truth which might cause incalculable transformations in social consciousness, which in turn might one day produce political debacles unpredictable in their consequences.

Vaclav Havel

The problems for any system of belief arise when fresh facts or well-supported theories run counter to the tenets of the tradition as currently formulated. To ignore these problems altogether is to display indifference to truth. To adhere unreasonably to the accepted formulation is to risk ossifying the tradition. To abandon it too readily may well be to forfeit the benefits to theory of a more tenacious policy, as well as making for practical ineffectiveness. In this sort of situation a tradition needs both strength and flexibility and it is natural for these virtues to become exemplified in different persons.

Believing in the Church

The Church can never be said to have apprehended the truth. Rather is the truth the divine action which apprehends the Church. Dimly it understands what it teaches. For the more the Church learns of God, the more it is aware of the incomprehensible mystery of His Being, in creation and in transcendence and on the Cross.

Michael Ramsey

Maybe one of the major pathologies of religious belief on our planet has been the insistence that firm faith commitment and intellectual certainty must go together. Perhaps that has led to the lamentable train of persecutions, hatreds, wars and arrogances that have characterised the history of religion, and still do. Where I perceive a clear truth which is absolutely certain, I may come to think that you must be blinded by evil, and your error has no excuse, no right to exist. I can, and perhaps should, eliminate it, and perhaps you with it. Seeing this with grief, I have no hesitation in praying for the end of certainty in religion, and the admission that we are at best seekers of truth blundering on the edges of infinity.

Keith Ward

Creeds are dangerous documents. As St. Hilary, one of Athanasius' supporters, wrote: 'We are compelled to attempt what is unattainable, to climb where we cannot reach, to speak

what we cannot utter. Instead of the bare adoration of faith we are compelled to entrust the deep things of religion to the perils of human expression.'
Michael Ramsey

If a sensitive enough instrument could be devised, every reciter of the creed could be shown to be meaning something different by it.
J.L. Houlden

... truth, which cannot be expressed in any other way than by myth and allegory, is like water that cannot be transported without a vessel.
Arthur Schopenhauer

The power of religious dogma, that has been inculcated early, is so great that it destroys conscience, and finally all compassion and sense of humanity.
Arthur Schopenhauer

God offers to every man the choice between truth and repose. Take which you will. You can never have both.
Ralph Waldo Emerson

Faith which does not doubt is dead faith.
Miguel de Unamuno

It is not like a child that I believe in Christ and confess Him. My hosanna has come forth from the crucible of doubt.
Fyodor Dostoyevsky

There are times when we must sink to the bottom of our misery to understand truth, just as we must descend to the bottom of a well to see the stars in broad daylight.
Vaclav Havel

By doubting we are led to inquire, by inquiring we perceive the truth.
Peter Abelard

I am not attempting here to discuss the difficulties attaching to Christian belief. I know that they are real and manifold. I am only pointing out that those who have encountered Christ and made a wholehearted response to that encounter have found an answer to the problem of man and truth. They have been given a faith which they do not have to carry, but which carries them. It is the testimony of Christians that amid all the uncertainties of relativism they have discovered that to which they may surrender themselves in complete trust. They have encountered a reality which gives them confidence that the universe is trustworthy. What they have known and experienced of love is something that they believe will hold firm in all the stresses and tests of life and prove stronger than death itself.

That is one answer to the problem of man and truth. I do not myself know of any other answer in which my mind can rest. But it is inherent in that answer, as I understand it, that the answer must vindicate itself in open and free discussion, that all formulations of the answer made by fallible men are necessarily defective and incomplete and are in constant need of correction and enrichment by the contribution of the experience of all sincere seekers after truth.

J.H. Oldham

Sometime, somewhere you take something to be the truth. If you cling to it so much, when the truth comes in person and knocks at your door, you will not open it.

The Buddha

I resolved that I would believe in Christ and take Him for my Master in whatever I did . . . that to disbelieve was as difficult as to believe; that there are mysteries either way, but that the best mystery was that which gave me Christ for a Master. When I had done this I felt a peace within me which I had never known before . . .

John Ruskin

The truth that makes us free is found only by the exercise of freedom.

Believing in the Church

Speaking the truth in love, we are to grow up in every way into him who is the head, into Christ.

Ephesians 4:15

17

THE CHURCH

So far from belief in the Christian creed being a precondition of membership (of the Church) it is one of the results of membership, one indeed which may take a whole lifetime to achieve. It is the end of a process, not the beginning.

The process begins with the natural growth – points of love present in every human being who has not been fatally distorted or mutilated by external forces. The dogmatic hurdles at the entrance to the church therefore succeed in doing only two things: they let in people who for the most part have made a purely mental and superficial assent to the formularies, and who then spend their lives putting on an act, an external and artificial mimicking of a way of life that is spontaneous or nothing, and they keep out a great many people in whom the root of love is growing and flowering but who for one reason or another cannot commit themselves sincerely to the full dogmatic faith of the Church.

In this way those inside are cut off from the very fellowship which would help them to mature in love, and those outside are denied the opportunity to move towards a real understanding of the faith. Everyone gets the worst of all possible worlds; and only an open church offers any hope of putting this right.

John Austin Baker

> Once I am sure there's nothing going on
> I step inside, letting the door thud shut.
> Another church: matting, seats, and stone,
> And little books; sprawling of flowers, cut
> For Sunday, brownish now; some brass and stuff
> Up at the holy end; the small neat organ;
> And a tense, musty, unignorable silence,

> Brewed God knows how long. Hatless, I take off
> My cycle-clips in awkward reverence...
>
> A serious house on serious earth it is,
> In whose blent air all our compulsions meet,
> Are recognised, and robed as destinies.
> And that much never can be obsolete,
> Since someone will forever be surprising
> A hunger in himself to be more serious,
> And gravitating with it to this ground,
> Which, he once heard, was proper to grow wise in,
> If only that so many dead lie round.
>
> *Philip Larkin*

When I think of the act of entering the Church as something imminent no thought causes me more pain than that of separating myself from the huge unhappy multitude of unbelievers.

I do not want to belong to a milieu, to live in a milieu where people say 'We' (*nous autres*) and be a part of that 'We', to find myself at home in any human society.

I would like to call your attention to one point. It is that there is an absolutely impassable barrier to the incarnation of Christianity. It is the use of two small words 'anathema sit' (let him be anathema). Not their existence, but the use that has been made of them. It is this also which prevents me from crossing the threshold of the Church. I remain on the side of everything that cannot enter the Church, that universal dustbin created by the use of those two little words.

Simone Weil

As a Roman Catholic I thank God for the heretics. Heresy is only another word for freedom of thought.

Graham Greene

The church's *defences* against modern thought are at the same time *gateways* for the entrance of modern politics. Knowing this, politicians invariably urge a simple populist faith upon the church. It will make her easier for them to control.

Don Cupitt

The life of the Christian Church bears too many of the scars of the triumphs of evil to permit us to be complacent. The catalogue of the victories of the prince of this world, in which Auschwitz is but the latest of his crimes, is saddeningly long.

'The conversion of Constantine which subjected the Eastern Church to the imperial power; the legitimation of persecution; the raising of the flesh to the rank of the Devil himself as the enemy of man, and the inhuman doctrine of predestination which the great Augustine bequeathed to the Western Church; the great schism between the East and West; the dissensions and corruption of medieval Christendom; the religious wars of the sixteenth and seventeenth centuries; the rejection of Christianity by the French Revolution and the instant corruption of the ideals of the revolutionaries themselves . . .' – the list is R.C. Zaehner's . . . Many Jews from far off days until now have rejected a Christ presented to them by this Church. Is it quite so certain that they were wrong to turn away from that face?

Alan Ecclestone

Although by the power of the Holy Spirit the Church has remained the faithful spouse of her Lord and has never ceased to be the sign of salvation on earth, still she is very well aware that among her members, both clerical and lay, some have been unfaithful to the Spirit of God during the course of many centuries. In the present age, too, it does not escape the Church how great a distance lies between the message she offers and the human failings of those to whom the gospel is entrusted.

Vatican II. The Church in the Modern World

Christian faith directly seeks the ultimate liberation and freedom of the children of God in the Kingdom, but it also includes historical liberation as an anticipation and concretization of that ultimate liberation.

The Church reaches out to them (the poor) directly, not through the state or the ruling classes. Thus, we are no longer speaking of a Church *for* the poor but rather of a Church *of* and *with* the poor.

Leonardo Boff

When the Church becomes poorer and loses her confidence in the efficiency of great material resources, she is on the road to renewal and will take many others, believers and non-believers, along with her. In the Church the power of material resources inspires fear. A powerful man inspires fear and, although he may indeed call himself a Christian, he does not awaken others to life in God; his faith loses its credibility. The same is true of the Church.

Roger Schutz

The way to call anyone into fellowship with us is, not to offer them service, which is liable to arouse the resistance of their pride, but to ask service from them. The Church is the only institution which exists for the benefit of those who are not its members.

William Temple

The Church matters not for itself, not for its paid-up members, but for what it says about everyone mattering, what it affirms about *all* – not merely believers – belonging to the family of humanity and being children of God.

Hugh Dawes

The state of the world's disorder festers in every continent. Even in a still relatively quiet Britain there is unemployment by the million, racial riots and a really profound sense of lostness. Yet the Church cannot witness effectively in regard to any of these things outside itself if its own institutions and contemporary insistences are flawed and unconvincing to its own members. Its service of witness depends upon its structures of ministry. Almost a whole generation – that of my nephews and nieces and their friends – has lost its Christian faith, and the sheer sense of the irrelevancy of ecclesiastical preoccupations has a great deal to do with it.

Adrian Hastings

A really free church will be a church whose power-structure has decayed because people no longer find difference offensive to them.

Don Cupitt

Kierkegaard's value to the Church today lies in giving vitality to the contemporary question first posed in the days of Paul;

what does it mean to become a Christian not in assent to a dogmatic proposition, but in response to the invitation of a suffering servant.

Andrew Cruickshank.

> A preaching that awakens,
> a preaching that enlightens,
>   as when a light turned on
>   awakens and annoys a sleeper –
> that is the preaching of Christ, calling:
>   Wake up! Be converted!
> That is the Church's authentic preaching.
> Naturally, such preaching must meet conflict.
>   must spoil what is miscalled prestige,
>   must disturb,
>   must be persecuted.
> It cannot get along with the powers of darkness and sin.
>
> *Oscar Romero*

Several clear messages for the Church emerge from these quotations from our modern prophets. They are, first, that she should welcome criticism and stop chasing heretics; that she needs to be open to those with a sincere desire to become disciples, but who cannot honestly believe or accept all her dogma; that she needs to abandon her reliance on great material resources: to become poorer and to be of and with the poor. These are formidable challenges. Can bishops, clergy and laity – the whole People of God – respond to Oscar Romero's rallying call: 'Wake up! Be converted!'

The choice between the open, diversified church and church behind institutional and mental barricades emerges yet more clearly as the supreme issue for the next century.

John Taylor

The Christian churches have too often made the test of faith assent to certain highly technical doctrines, and neglected the really important matter of how much love, reconciliation and joy is growing in human lives.

Keith Ward

18

THE BIBLE

In almost all parts of the Bible we can feel ourselves in touch with religious personalities, some of them displaying exceptional inspiration, all of them men of insight and sincerity. They write out of their experience of God in the Soul, or of God's dealings in what happened to them and their people. Because they were 'men of God', their experience is a valid representation of divine reality. It profits us as we 'live ourselves into it'. (*Sich hineinleben*).

C.H. Dodd

The Bible has suffered from being treated too much as a source of information. The traditional theory valued it as giving authoritative information, in the form of dogma, upon matters known only by special revelation. The critical method has too often issued in treating it as a collection of information for the antiquary. Its place as a whole is rather with the masterpieces of poetry, drama and philosophy, that is, the literature which does not so much impart information but stirs the deeper levels of personality.

C.H. Dodd

It being the professed design of the Scripture to teach us such things as we neither see nor know of ourselves, its style and manner must be such as are no where else to be found. It must abound with figurative expressions; it cannot proceed without them: and if we descend to an actual examination of particulars, we find it assisting and leading our faculties forward: by an application of all visible objects to a figurative use; from the glorious orb which shines in the firmament to a grain of seed which is buried in the earth. In this sort of language did our blessed Saviour instruct his hearers; always referring them to such objects as were familiar to their senses, that they might see the propriety and feel the force of his doctrines. This method he observed, not in compliance with any customary speech peculiar to the Eastern people, but consulting the exigence of human nature, which is everywhere the same.

To those who understand it, all nature speaks the same language with revelation: what the one teaches in words the other confirms with signs . . . If Christ is called the *true bread*, or the *true light*, or the *true vine*, and the talents or gifts of God's grace are the *true riches*, etc., then the objects of sense, without this their spirit and signification, are in themselves mere image and delusion; and the whole life of man in this world is but a shadow.

William Jones

The metaphor that Christ is the 'light of the world' changes not merely the way in which we are to understand Christ, but also the way we understand *light*.

Stephen Prickett

The language of signs is essentially that of poetry, both disclosing and *creating.*

Something is happening at two levels. That is the discovery you make, or rather which dawns gradually upon you, as you read John's gospel. He is describing the same events at two levels – what men and women are doing on the physical level, and at the same time what God is doing on the level of Spirit.

Things are happening on the physical level which you could see by the light of the sun and which a modern television team might record with a camera. But at the same time, through the earthly reality of these physical events another kind of reality is revealing itself. This you cannot see by the light of the sun, but only by another light, which shines on the events and on you yourself. It opens your eyes, and shows you everything 'in a new light'.

Stephen Verney

To regard myths literally is to mistake the denotation for the connotation.

Joseph Campbell

Metaphor may be seen as the bridge between language, nature, history and their spirit and signification as 'signs'.
  This is nothing new as the following quotation written in the 14th Century clearly shows:

... take care not to interpret physically what is intended spiritually even though material expressions are used, like 'up, down, out, behind, before, this side, that side'. The most spiritual thing imaginable, if we are to speak of it at all ... must always be spoken of in physical words. But what of it? Are we therefore to understand it physically? Indeed not, but spiritually.

The Cloud of Unknowing

It has been suggested that the story of the feeding of the five thousand could originally have been a parable (like the jar of meal and cruse of oil in I Kings 17) illustrating the fact that, in spiritual matters, the more you give the more you receive and that the supply is never exhausted.

It is characteristic of the Old Testament writers that they never failed to use the dark background of human depravity to throw up the ever-brightening picture of the Divine perfection, and especially to illustrate God's unfailing faithfulness.

E. Griffith-Jones

The Epistle to the Hebrews sets forth not only the essential idea of scripture but the method of it; in other words the method of divine education by which men in the old time were enabled to enter into this idea, to see how it must be realised.

F.D. Maurice

It is by making what is first and oldest new and contemporary that we become creative.

Laurens van der Post

A symbol that can only mean one thing is not fulfilling the function of a symbol.
Edward Robinson

Understanding of the Bible over the centuries has been hindered both by imagination undisciplined by critical awareness on the one hand, and on the other by literalists unable to see that literalism diminishes and impoverishes the Bible precisely because it denies imagination which alone is creative. There is no one 'correct' interpretation of the Bible or its parts; what should inform our minds, and therefore our culture, is the cumulative effect of the multitude of different facets revealed through the imagination of countless individuals, though some of these will obviously be more important than others.

Take not, oh Lord, our literal sense, Lord, in thy great,
Unbroken speech our limping metaphor translate.
C.S. Lewis

Newman supported me in my belief that the New Testament was addressed to the Imagination. It was first of all a record of facts, which were presented to the mind in the most vivid, imaginative way. It was a poetic history, and, in addition, the doctrine of the New Testament was presented entirely in imaginative terms. There were no abstract philosophical concepts; all was expressed in the richly symbolic terms of poetry and imagination. Christ spoke of himself in terms of the Messiah and his kingdom, two concepts of infinite imaginative significance. He compared himself to a Bridegroom, to a

Shepherd, to a Vine. Even the terms in which he spoke of his relation to God were profoundly symbolic; he spoke of God as his Father, of himself as the Son, of the Spirit which he would send. Now these terms set forth the Object of faith, as Newman showed, in the way which makes the deepest impression on the mind and nourishes love and devotion, but they are lacking in precision.

Bede Griffiths

Newman believed that it was inevitable that attempts should be made to give these poetic terms more exact expression. In his own words, 'What was an impression on the imagination became a system or creed in the reason'. It is perhaps legitimate to ask whether this does not involve a misunderstanding of the very nature of poetry and symbol which can never be given an exact or precise expression in the sense of having only one clear meaning.

There is no starting point anywhere which is not already an interpretation and therefore questionable, and there can be no final interpretation which neither calls for nor permits any further comment.

Don Cupitt

> Both read the Bible day and night,
> But thou read'st black where I read white.

William Blake

Education in general and religious education in particular must be rich in human awareness, beauty, and symbolism for men to be able to read the Bible with full appreciation.

Gabriel Moran

In the Christian era the phrase 'word of God' refers first of all to the Son, the personal Word who comes from the Father. The Bible is also in some sense the 'word of God' but by considering the Scriptures in relation to Christ we come to realize that the 'Word of God' always come to us received and incarnated in the human.

Gabriel Moran

A divine Truth panoplied in power, triumphant over the world and conquering souls, would not be consonant with the freedom of man's spirit, and so the mystery of Golgotha is the mystery of liberty . . . Every time in history that man has tried to turn crucified Truth into coercive truth he has betrayed the fundamental principle of Christ.

Nicholas Berdyaev

In the Bible God's commands never override human freedom to disobey, rebel and take the consequences. In spite of God's command not to eat of the fruit of the tree Eve 'took of its fruit and ate; and she also gave some to her husband and he ate'. The people of Israel were 'a nation of rebels'; when the prophets speak to them they 'hear or refuse to hear'. The contemporaries of Jesus may refuse an invitation to a dance or a party; no-one will compel them to come. The prodigal son is free to go his way, and free to return home. The rich young aristocrat is told what he must do, but is free to reject the advice he is given. Judas is free to betray Jesus, the authorities (religious and political) to crucify him.

This freedom is neither given nor accepted without suffering. In the Bible man's freedom implies the vulnerability of God and of his representatives. The suffering servant described in the fifty-third chapter of Isaiah may be identified with Israel, or Jesus, or both; what is significant is that God's servant is depicted not as one who ruthlessly crushes his enemies with overwhelming power, but as one who is himself despised and rejected, wounded, not for his own, but for our transgressions – suffering that we may be free.

And he said to them, 'O foolish men, and slow of heart to believe all that the prophets have spoken! Was it not necessary that the Christ should suffer these things and enter into his glory?' And beginning with Moses and all the prophets, he interpreted to them in all the scriptures the things concerning himself.

Luke 24:25–27

It is dangerous to believe that one has a guaranteed truth in some ancient document, which is certain, unchangeable and ultimately authoritative in every detail. It is dangerous in a number of ways. First, it is simply false to think that a belief is certain when it is not (when competent, informed judges reject it). Since religion usually claims to be concerned with truth, it is a pity to force believers to accept such a basic falsehood. Second, such a view makes faith a matter of assenting to a set of stateable propositions about ancient history. But the danger is that this misses the true character of faith. Faith should not be a matter of assenting, by an act of will, to more or less improbable propositions. Faith should be a matter of a growth in love and understanding evoked and empowered by the divine love itself.

Keith Ward

19

SACRAMENT

If we receive in the Eucharist the Lord's body and thereby the pledge of eternal life, it must also be said, . . . that the effect of the Sacrament – namely spiritual union with God in Jesus Christ and his grace – may occasionally occur more radically at points in our life where there is no Sacrament.

To begin with, the whole liturgy as such . . . belongs to the dimension of the *sign*, of what in this sense is 'Sacramental'; and what is signified by the sign, however intimately connected with the sign itself, nevertheless belongs to another dimension. The Sacrament (sacramentum) and the 'thing signified' by the Sacrament (*res Sacramenti*) are simply not identical . . .

When a person succeeds, in a situation which God controls and we do not, in definitively giving up his whole nature unselfishly into the infinite ineffable mystery of God, in letting himself fall into this abyss of God, which is also precisely the abyss of Jesus' death – in certain circumstances, in a radical unselfish encounter with his neighbour – this is the summit of the authentic reality mediated through the Sacrament.

Karl Rahner

All forms of Christian worship, all forms of Christian discipline, have this (mutual indwelling) as their object. Whatever leads to this is good; whatever hinders this is bad; whatever does not bear on this is futile. This is the life of the Christian: Abide in me and I in you. All truth and depth of devotion, all effectiveness in service, spring from this.

William Temple

Through the Sacramental medium of common circumstance we hear the voice of the Eternal Word, and hearing are created.

For the Eternal Word is not a cult-object in the possession of the churches, nor an esoteric device traded by the mystagogues. It is the creative voice that speaks by means of anything or everything which impinges upon us in the ordinary business of our daily lives.

H.A. Williams

The martyr signposts (and so is in himself a sacrament) the direction in which language which speaks of the absolute can be meaningful.

Leonardo Boff

In the other Gospel accounts of the Last Supper, Christ takes the bread, blesses and breaks it, saying, 'Take and eat: this is me given for you. Do this in my memory' The life of the Father, expressed in the human Jesus, is a life that is given for us – 'All I have is yours.' 'Do this in memory' is not an instruction to perform a ritual, but a request to let the life of Christ, and therefore of the Father, a life of sharing, become our life.

As the life of Christ takes hold on us, our lives will be transformed from being lives of self-protection, self-care, self-cultivation, into lives given for others, because God, the God of compassion, will have taken possession of our being.

Gerard W. Hughes

Every celebration of the Eucharist is a celebration of the life, passion, death and resurrection of Christ in which all creation is involved and taken up. . . . The same God who manifested himself in the historical Jesus once-for-all is still giving himself to us in love through the signs and symbols of bread and wine. God is not time-and space-conditioned.

The Eucharist is given to us so that Christ's presence may be real in the lives of his people, a presence living in our attitudes and values, in our thinking, speaking and the style of life we choose to live. It is important that we should show great reverence to Christ in the sacrament of the Eucharist, but it is even more important that we should let his presence be real in our lives, for that is the reason he has given us the Eucharist, 'so that you may copy what I have done to you'.

Gerard W. Hughes

At the Church Leaders Conference at Selly Oak in 1972 Cardinal Heenan propounded the odd opinion that inter-communion could be permissible in a concentration camp, but not elsewhere. The conference chairman commented that we should then pray for a multiplication of concentration camps. Can only concentration camps and hurricanes make the crooked ways straight? Yet are we not already, if we had but the eyes to see, in an emergency quite comparable to either?

Adrian Hastings

The Sacrament is central in Christianity as a sign, but it is a sign of something beyond itself and, as Karl Rahner claims, the summit of the authentic reality mediated through the Sacrament may be reached where there is no Sacrament: for example, in a radical unselfish encounter with our neighbour.

Harry Williams stresses the sacramental medium of the ordinary business of our daily lives and this is spelled out more fully by Gerard Hughes.

Adrian Hastings raises the crucial question: if inter-communion is permissible in a concentration camp, why is it not permissible in a world full of violence, persecution, hatred, famine and disease? Is inter-communion a means towards unity or only an expression of unity once it has been reached? Does unity mean institutional unity or a unity of interpretation? If the former, is it not comparatively superficial? If the latter, may it not be postponed until we meet in heaven to discover with embarrassed laughter how myopic we were here on earth!

Confronted by the challenge of the world, the difference between Christians with episcopal and non-episcopal ministries seems almost blasphemously irrelevant. The question has been put like this: 'On the march to Selma, would you or would you not have been prepared to share communion with or take communion from Martin Luther King?'. . . . The impatience of so many today at fencing of altars springs, I believe, from a high doctrine of the kingdom, of the priority of involvement in the world . . .

John A.T. Robinson

The Word of God in Scripture is a special sacrament of his presence just as real, though different in form, as his presence in the Eucharist.

Gerard W. Hughes

For Newman, the Church lived not through its theology, but in its symbols and sacraments. 'Christ lives, to our imagination, by his visible symbols'. – not simply sacraments but by the whole complex web of visual iconography and literary metaphor which has grown from the Bible and the associated traditions of the Church. It is to these things, which appeal not merely to our intellects but to our imagination that we can give 'real' as opposed to 'notional' assent.

Stephen Prickett

All of the Christian mysteries are sacramental mysteries because they are communicated and made present through human or cosmic mediation.

Leonardo Boff

To say that God makes a world is to say that God makes matter the bearer of spirit. It is characteristic of human beings, made in God's image, to endow matter with meaning: in artistic creation, in ceremonial, and not least in everyday activities, such as the giving of gifts . . . Each human being is a kind of walking sacrament: which is what we properly mean by saying that human life is 'sacred'.

Helen Oppenheimer

In the agricultural (as opposed to desert) tradition of the Old Testament wine was the symbol of joy in living and blood the symbol of life, the offering of blood symbolizing the offering of life. At the Last Supper Jesus brings together these two symbols so that the offering of life is the fullness of joy: the blood and the wine are one. 'This (wine) is my blood'.

The mutual sacrifice which expresses mutual *love* is the most joyous thing in the world. It is the life of Heaven.

William Temple

20

SIN

> My Emanation far within
> Weeps incessantly for my sin
> *William Blake*

In Blake the 'Emanation' may be identified with the visionary self – the self which is capable of 'seeing' in a spiritual sense.

He who waits to be righteous before he enters into the Saviour's kingdom, the Divine Body, will never enter there.

> Each Man is in his Spectre's power
> Until the arrival of that hour
> When his Humanity awake
> And cast his own Spectre into the Lake
> *William Blake*

The Spectre is the deadening influence which hinders the awakening of Imagination, the ability to see.

Blake identifies man's humanity with the Divine Imagination, and the ultimate purpose of Imagination is to create in us 'the Spirit of Jesus' which he described as 'continual forgiveness of sin'.

But what kind of forgiveness?

I 'forgive and forget'. I call it forgiveness when I omit the actual execution of revenge. I forgive by relegating the subject of my forgiveness to a rank of inferiority far below my magnanimous self.

Or I forgive conditionally . . . Great honour has conditional forgiveness. It is a bulwark of the church. It is divine in the eyes of the law. It commends itself to every reasonable man as the limit of human charity.

Thus my highest conception of forgiveness appears as a contract of which the offender shall pay the stamp and lawyer's fee. There does not seem to be anything particularly divine about it. Indeed it looks unmistakably like self-justification.

The Spirit of Satan is continual self-justification.
Max Plowman on William Blake

One of the signs that we really have lost a sense of sin and a spirit of repentance is the selective nature of our moral teaching, its individualist emphasis, which ignores our corporate responsibility for the sin of the world, and its condemnatory tone.

Selective morality, which emphasizes, for example, the sacredness of property rights and punishes any infringement more severely than infringement of human rights, or which emphasizes sexual morality but remains blind to, or silent about, the destruction of human life through financial greed or false patriotism, can be a subtle way of protecting ourselves from God and from his demands, and is a sign of our failure to repent.

Jesus sums up his own teaching in the first of the beatitudes: 'Blessed (that is, 'blissfully happy') are you who are poor: yours is the kingdom of heaven.' Blissfully happy are you who know your own emptiness and throw yourselves on the mercy of God. The opposite state is described in Luke's Gospel: 'But alas for you who are rich: you are having your consolation now.' 'Rich' refers not only to material possessions, but to that attitude of mind and heart which finds its ultimate security in anything that is not God. That is why religious people, closed in their own religiosity, are greater sinners than 'the tax gatherers and prostitutes'. Sin is destructive of human life. It is worth noting that the most violent conflicts today are among people with strong religious beliefs, convinced that God is on their side as they murder their enemies – in Northern Ireland, Lebanon, Iran and Iraq, South Africa.

Sin is the refusal to let God be God.

Knowing our sinfulness and repenting is a lifelong, continual process. We can never reach a stage before death when we no longer need repentance, because there are layers upon layers of consciousness within us, and each moment of existence can reveal these layers, if we let it, and show us the depth of the tendency within us to refuse to let God be God.

Gerard W. Hughes

'Mammon' and riches mean not only money and material possessions, but stand for any idol in our lives, any created thing which becomes the focus of our praise, reverence and service. Mammon can be an ideology of any 'ism' which we allow to possess us. Mammon can be a patriotism, my country right or wrong, or it can be the way in which we practise religion, when our dedication becomes dedication to particular structures or formulations of the Christian message, and their preservation in the form familiar to us becomes more important than the worship and service of God, the God of mystery and of love, before whom all human structures must be provisional. 'The Sabbath is made for man, not man for the Sabbath,' as Jesus said to the Pharisees.

Gerard W. Hughes

Cruelty, indeed, cruelty, for instance, once you learn it, you may find if difficult to wean yourself thereof. Just as once you learn to swim in the river, you never forget how, or so I have been told by those who swim in the river, and about cruelty, or evil, or the doubt in man, no, a person cannot be cruel by turns, or evil every third time, or suspicious of his fellow man every fourth, as though evil were an object man carried with him, to take out and use when he pleases, or leave in his pocket if he so prefers, and peace be unto you, my soul. No, I am certain that you, too, have witnessed the fact that cruelty, suspicion, and evil infect all of life. Once you open a loophole for them, they infest the soul like mildew.

David Grossman

When thou attackest the roots of sin, fix thy thought more upon the God whom thou desirest than upon the sin which thou abhorest.

Walter Hylton

The sinner of to-day is the saint of to-morrow.

Meister Eckhart

Seldom does the faineant become the Saint; the vigorous sinner often. *Pecca fortiter* (despite Luther) is no maxim of spirituality; but he that sins strongly has the stuff of sanctity, rather than the languid sinner. The energies need turning Godward; but the energies are most necessary.

Francis Thompson

I am not a good man, but I do know about goodness.

Patrick White

Saul owed his conversation neither to true love, nor to true faith, nor to any other truth. It was solely his hatred of the Christians that set him upon the road to Damascus, and to that decisive experience which was to decide the whole course of his life. He was brought to this experience by following with conviction the course in which he was most completely mistaken.

C.G. Jung

Our delight in pursuing the bad comes from our belief that it is the good.

Jalalu D-Din Rumi

Two men went up into the temple to pray, one a Pharisee and the other a tax-collector. The Pharisee stood and prayed thus with himself, 'God, I thank thee that I am not like other men, extortioners, unjust, adulterers, or even like this tax collector. I fast twice a week, I give tithes of all that I get'. But the tax collector, standing far off, would not even lift up his eyes to heaven, but beat his breast, saying, 'God, be merciful to me a sinner!' I tell you this man went down to his house justified rather than the other; for every one who exalts himself will be humbled, but he who humbles himself will be exalted.

Luke 18:10 – 14

>Now is my way clear, now is the meaning plain:
>Temptation shall not come in this kind again.
>The last temptation is the greatest treason:
>To do the right deed for the wrong reason.

T.S. Eliot

The supreme test is not to be conscientious up to the measure of rules of universal application, but to be continually in search of a more penetrating discernment.

John Oman

Servant of God has chance of greater sin
And sorrow, than the man who serves a king.
For those who serve the greater cause may make the cause serve them,
Still doing right: and striving with political men
May make that cause political, not by what they do
But by what they are.

T.S. Eliot

He knew himself to be so incorruptible that he denied himself no crime.

André Maurois (of Robespierre)

If Blake's identification of sin with continual self-justification strikes home to us as individuals with our conditional forgiveness, does it not also apply to rulers of both church and state? If we do not believe that we are justified by God, we have to justify ourselves. This is where the doctrine of Justification by Faith has its bearing in our modern predicament. Those who do not believe they are justified by trust in God seek to justify themselves by achievement of one sort or another – in their career, in politics, even in the church: they tend to become dogmatic and self-righteous. This is a point T.S. Eliot brings out in Becket's struggle with the tempters in 'Murder in the Cathedral'; Hans Küng also makes it forcibly in the following quotation. The opposite of sin (self-justification) is faith – what Küng frequently refers to as 'basic trust.'

What is important in the last resort is for man to recognize the limitations of thinking in terms of achievement, to break through the pressure of achievement and the obsession with achievement, to place his life on a new foundation a new basic attitude, a different 'awareness', making possible for him a truly human existence, a new freedom.

If man binds himself in faith alone to the one Absolute, to the one true God, who is not identical with any finite reality, then he becomes free in regard to all finite values, goods, powers, which preserve their true – that is, relative – importance.

Hans Küng

We have to absorb evil in an excess of trust and faith.
Teilhard de Chardin

> The manifold delight I learn to take in earthly things
> can never drive me from my Love.
> for in the nobility of creatures,
> In their beauty and their usefulness,
> I will love God –
> and not myself!
> *Mechtild of Magdeburg*

As a rule it was the pleasure haters who became unjust.
W.H. Auden

21

JUDGEMENT

I have set before you life and death, blessing and curse, therefore choose life!
Deut 30:19

For I was hungry and you gave me no food, I was thirsty and you gave me no drink. I was a stranger and you did not welcome me, naked and you did not clothe me, sick and in prison and you did not visit me. Then they also will answer, 'Lord, when did we see thee hungry or thirsty or a stranger or naked or sick or in prison, and did not minister to thee?' Then he will answer them, 'Truly, I say to you, as you did it not to one of the least of these, you did it not to me.'
Matthew 25:42–45

This passage seems to make it clear that the ultimate test is not a matter of belief or church membership but essentially practical:

The ultimate criterion of a person's Christian spirit is not theory but practice: not how he thinks of teachings, dogmas, interpretations, but how he acts in ordinary life.
Hans Küng

There is no way out of the human situation – not nuclear defence, not economic progress, not a political system. In each human heart the choice of good and evil must be made. There is no other way but a repentant return of our consciousness to the Creator of all. When He leaves us we die, yet in God the highest gifts of the human spirit may become manifest and in that alone is hope for the future.
Alexander Solzhenitsyn

> No, when the fight begins within himself,
> A man's worth something. God stoops O'er his head,
> Satan looks up between his feet – both tug –
> He's left, himself in the middle: the soul wakes
> And grows. Prolong that battle through his life!
> Never leave growing till the life to come!
>
> *Robert Browning*

At the end of the day we always go where our whole weight carries us.

Antoine St. Exupéry

No man can shelter himself behind the triumphant will of God: rather, when it is once perceived, he comes under judgement and enters into a condition of shattering confusion – from which he can never escape.

Kart Barth

> Would that you knew what the steep way is!
> It is the freeing of the slave,
> Or giving food in the hungry day
> To an orphan near of kin,
> Or to some needy soul in his distress.
> Such are believers indeed:
> Patience and mercy are their counsel,
> Their counsel to each other.
>
> *Surah of The Land*
> *The Qur'an*

Have mercy on me, O Beneficent One, I was angered for I had no shoes: Then I met a man who had no feet.

Chinese saying

Judgement is not a popular theme in religious circles to-day. That is understandable because the theme, and the threat, have been too lightly used in the interest of ecclesiastical or clerical power. That danger will always exist where human nature predominates over the mind of Christ. Yet, when it is divorced from power-seeking there is a proper use of this theme. Either our attitudes and actions from day to day are meaningless, or they carry some ultimate meaning for our lives and so determine our destiny. If we choose life with meaning then the last judgement 'takes place every day' (Camus). It is a matter of life or death, or, as Eliot suggests in Little Gidding *a choice between different kinds of death, one of which leads to life.*

What do you think? A man had two sons; and he went to the first and said, 'Son, go and work in the vineyard today.' And he answered, 'I will not'; but afterward he repented and went. And he went to the second and said the same; and he answered, 'I go, sir,' but did not go. Which of the two did the will of his father?

Matthew 21:28

Judge not, that you be not judged.

Matthew 7:1

Don't wait for the last Judgement. It takes place every day.

Albert Camus

God did not send his son into the *kosmos* to judge the *kosmos* in the sense of condemning it: nevertheless judgement inevitably followed from his coming. For when the light shines, some people scuttle away into cover of darkness, while others expose themselves to the light which they need for their growth, and to see where they are going.

Stephen Verney

> The dove descending breaks the air
> With flame of incandescent terror
> Of which the tongues declare
> The one discharge from sin and error.
> The only hope, or else despair
>   Lies in the choice of pyre or pyre –
>   To be redeemed from fire by fire.
>
> Who then devised the torment? Love.
> Love is the unfamiliar Name
> Behind the hands that wove
> The intolerable shirt of flame
> Which human power cannot remove.
>   We only live, only suspire
>   Consumed by either fire or fire

T.S. Eliot

Lord, have mercy upon us.
Christ, have mercy upon us.
Lord, have mercy upon us.

22

FORGIVENESS

'Lord, how often shall my brother sin against me, and I forgive him? As many as seven times?' Jesus said to him, 'I do not say to you seven times, but seventy times seven.'

Matthew 18:21–22

If forgiveness meant letting off the criminal it would be a violation of the love-commandment. We have no right to be turning other people's cheeks, leaving other people's children to be raped or lonely old ladies to be beaten up, allowing thieves and murderers to run loose. But in Christian theology, forgiveness does not mean being let off the consequences. Forgiveness means reconciliation.

F.R. Barry

How had the impossible thing happened to them or begun to happen? . . . His very crucifixion, which had so scandalized and scattered them, had a great deal to do with it, and was indeed at the heart of the secret. For now, looking back, they could see that this was actually the love of God dealing with the sins of men, offering them forgiveness and a new beginning if only they would come and accept it. That was what had broken down their self-centred pride and made them willing to come back into fellowship, not as good and worthy men who had a right, but as sinners all alike in need of mercy.

Donald Baillie

The guilt of an action is directly proportionate to the extent to which the doer knows that it is wrong; its injurious effect, however upon his moral character is inversely proportionate to the extent to which he regrets it.

B.H. Streeter

While God does not and man does not demand repentance as a condition for bestowing pardon, repentance remains an essential condition for receiving it.

Dorothy Sayers

The absolutely unpardonable thing was not his concern for the sick, the cripples, the lepers, the possessed; not the way he put up with women and children around him; nor even his partisanship for the poor, humble people. The real trouble was that he got involved with moral failures, with obviously irreligious and immoral people: people morally and politically suspect, so many dubious, obscure, abandoned hopeless types existing as an ineradicable evil on the fringe of every society. This was the real scandal. Did he really have to go so far? This attitude in practice is notably different from the general behaviour of religious people.

Hans Küng

> Wilt thou forgive that sinne where I begunne,
> Which is my sin, though it were done before?
> Wilt thou forgive those sinnes, through which I runne,
> And do run still: though still I do deplore?
>
> Wilt thou forgive that sinne by which I have wonne
> Others to sinne? and, made my sinne their doore?
> Wilt thou forgive that sinne which I did shunne
> A yeare, or two: but wallowed in, a score?

John Donne

I felt my heart strangely warmed. I felt I did trust in Christ, Christ alone, for salvation: and an assurance was given me that he had taken away my sins, even mine, and saved me from the law of sin and death.

John Wesley

> The Christian trumpets loud proclaim
> Thro' all the world in Jesus' name
> Mutual forgiveness of each Vice,
> And oped the Gates of Paradise.

William Blake

The Glory of Christianity is To Conquer by Forgiveness.
William Blake

> Tender and compassionate is the Lord,
>   slow to anger and full of love
> Not for all time does He accuse,
>   not forever does He keep His anger,
> not according to our failings has He dealt with us,
>   not according to our deceit has He treated us.
>
> As high as the sky over the earth,
>   so great is His love over those who fear Him:
> as far as the east from the west,
>   so far has He taken our misdeeds from us.

Psalm 103

In the popular mind forgiveness simply means letting off. In terms of criminal justice that would be 'a violation of the love commandment' (F.R. Barry) In Christian terms forgiveness does not mean being let off the consequences of sin: it means breaking through the entail of evil upon evil by costly reconciliation and therefore 'to conquer by forgiveness'.

The sole moral demand is sincerity, for no restoration is possible till we come to ourselves, and arise and go to our Father and say we have sinned, but it is vain to demand sincerity unless, when we go to our Father, we find more than condonation. Only because faith in Christ is the discovery of something more, does it justify. In itself, and merely as an inward grace, faith, no more than any other state of mind, effects pardon by legal merit. Not faith, but the love of God it trusts, speaks peace; and it does so, because faith in it is not of ourselves, but is the gift of God, the manifestation of what we may call an atoning order, understood by the sufferings of Christ and our partaking of them.

John Oman

Children begin by loving their parents; after a time they judge them; rarely, if ever, do they forgive them.

Oscar Wilde

The quality of mercy is not strain'd
It droppeth as the gentle rain from heaven
Upon the place beneath: it is twice bless'd:
It blesseth him that gives and him that takes:
'Tis mightiest in the mightiest: it becomes
The throned monarch better than his crown;
It is an attribute of God himself,
And earthly power doth then show likest God's
When mercy seasons justice . . .
. . . consider this,
That in the course of justice none of us
Should see salvation: we do pray for mercy,
And that same prayer doth teach us all to render
The deeds of mercy.
William Shakespeare

. . . of each story in the Gospels, we should ask, not 'Did it happen so?' but, 'What was it written to teach in the community who read it?' Was it not a story, based indeed on a remembered and beloved life, but meant to evoke the present experience of forgiveness for those who had never known Jesus in the flesh?
Keith Ward

Therefore I tell you, her sins, which are many, are forgiven, for she loved much; but he who is forgiven little, loves little.
Luke 7:47

23

GRACE

If men presume to claim for themselves upon the basis of the covenant some relationship with God other than that of the sinner needing God's grace, the covenant has been perverted . . . there is no law in His Kingdom save the law of pure grace. That is why they come from east and west to sit down with Abraham and Isaac, while the sons of the Kingdom are cast out, for the sons of the Kingdom have no place there unless they are willing to sit down with all whom the Lord of the feast shall call, and to receive His mercy in exactly the same way as the publicans and sinners.

Lesslie Newbigin

The muscular effort of the peasant pulls out the weeds, but only the sun and water make the wheat grow.

In salvation there is an effortless ease that is more difficult for us to accept than any kind of effort.

Simone Weil

Is the rule no longer to hold that the sinner must first make an effort, do penance, then receive grace? Is this whole system to lose its force? Must it not be made completely clear – as in the Old Testament books of Deuteronomy and Chronicles – that fidelity to the law is rewarded by God and lawlessness punished? According to this friend of tax collectors and sinners, is God, the holy God, supposed to forgive sinners as such, the unholy? But such a God would be a God of sinners: a God who loves sinners more than the righteous.

Here, clearly, the very foundations of religion are being shaken. Traitors, swindlers and adulterers are put in the right as against the devout and righteous. The depraved good-for-nothing is preferred to his brother who has worked hard at home. The hated foreigner – and, what is more, a heretic – is set up as an example to the natives.

Will not someone who is so sympathetic to outlaws and lawless men also break the law himself? Will he not fail to observe both ritual and disciplinary regulations, as these are set down according to God's commandment and the tradition of the Fathers? This is a fine purity of heart! Feasting instead of fasting! Man the measure of God's commandments! Celebration instead of punishment! Under these curcumstances it is not surprising if prostitutes and swindlers are supposed to enter God's kingdom before the devout, unbelievers from all parts before the children of the kingdom. What kind of lunatic justice is this which in fact abolishes all sacred standards and reverses all order of rank, making the last first and the first last? What kind of naive and dangerous love is this, which does not know its limits: the frontiers between fellow countrymen and foreigners, party members and non-members, between neighbours and distant people, between honorable and dishonorable callings, between moral and immoral, good and bad people? As if dissociation were not absolutely necessary here. As if we ought not to judge in these cases. As if we could always forgive in these circumstances.

Yes, Jesus did go so far: we may forgive, endlessly forgive, seven and seventy times. And all sins – except the sin against the Holy Spirit, against the reality of God himself, when the sinner does not want to be forgiven. Evidently an opportunity is offered to everyone, independently of social, ethnic, politico-religious divisions. And the sinner is accepted even before he repents. First comes grace, then the achievement. The sinner who has deserved every punishment is freely pardoned: he need only acknowledge the act of grace. Forgiveness is granted to him, he need only accept the gift and repent. This is a real amnesty – gratis. He need only live confidently in virtue of this grace. Grace then counts before law or, better, what holds is the law of grace. Only in this way is a new, higher righteousness possible. It begins with unconditional forgiveness: the sole condition is trust inspired by faith or trusting faith: the sole conclusion to be drawn is the generous granting of forgiveness to others. Anyone who is permitted to live, being forgiven in great things, should not refuse forgiveness in little things.

Hans Küng

Sometimes a wave of light breaks into our darkness, and it is as though a voice were saying: 'You are accepted. You are accepted by that which is greater than you, and the name of which you do not know. Do not ask for that name now; perhaps you will find it later. Do not try to do anything now: perhaps later you will do much. Do not seek for anything; do not perform anything. Simply accept the fact that you are accepted!' When that happens to us, we experience grace, and reconciliation bridges the gulf of estrangement.

Paul Tillich

It is the most worship that a solemn King or a great Lord may do a poor servant if he will be homely with him . . . Then thinketh this poor creature thus: And what might this noble Lord do of more worship and joy to me than to show me that am so simple this marvellous homeliness? Soothely it is more joy and pleasance to me than (if) he gave me great gifts and were himself strange in manner.

Thus it fareth with our Lord Jesus and with us. For verily it is the most joy that may be, as to my sight, that he that is highest and mightiest, noblest and worthiest, is lowest and meekest, homeliest and most courteous: and truly and verily this marvellous joy shall be shewn us all when we see Him.

Julian of Norwich

Grace is indeed needed to turn a man into a saint; and he who doubts it does not know what a saint or a man is.
Blaise Pascal

Jesus was a revolutionary – not, of course, in the modern violent sense of the word – but in the sense that he turned upside down the conventional view that repentance must come first and only then acceptance and forgiveness. The Jewish authorities believed that such a teaching undermined the Law and probably that was the most convincing reason for their opposition to him.

Let us admit that, for the most part, we still find this teaching revolutionary and, though we may pay lip service to it, find it unacceptable as a guide for our daily life. Jesus claimed that he did not come to destroy the Law but to fulfil it, and in the Sermon on the Mount, gave a number of examples of the way his teaching fulfilled the Law: to be rid of hatred is the fulfilment of the law against murder; to be rid of lust is the fulfilment of the law against adultery; to be honest is the fulfilment of the law against breaking oaths; to return good for evil is the fulfilment of the law limiting revenge; to love your enemies is an extension of the law to love your neighbour. But you cannot legislate for inward attitudes.

Paul had to grapple with this question of the Law and the Spirit which was a major problem for Jewish converts to Christianity. In his letter to the Romans he says the Law left people with a sense of guilt and fear ('condemnation') because they could never fully keep the Law: only grace (or unconditional forgiveness), when accepted with joy and gratitude, brings us into 'the glorious freedom of the children of God'.

IV
LOVE

24

FAITH

Yet even at the last the security which we seek is of faith and not of knowledge; it is not won by intellectual grasp but by personal loyalty; and its test is not in logic only, but in life.

William Temple

When all the guarantees, supports and bridges by which we strive to secure our life break down, when we lose all the ground from under our feet and sink into complete unconsciousness, from which we can no longer relate to any of our fellow human beings and none of them can relate to us, then faith becomes total, then it is revealed as what it always is or should be by its very nature: *reliance on God alone* and consequently faith in life and death.

Heinz Zahrnt

What is it that ultimately counts in human life? That, healthy or sick, able to work or unable to work, strong in achievement or weak in achievement, accustomed to success or passed over by success, guilty or innocent, a person clings unswervingly and unshakably, not only at the end but throughout his whole life, to that trust which always in the New Testament goes by the name of *faith*.

Hans Küng

> Pure faith indeed – you know not what you ask!
> Naked belief in God the Omnipotent,
> Omniscient, Omnipresent, sears too much
> The sense of conscious creatures to be borne.
> It were the seeing Him, no flesh shall dare.
> Some think, Creation's meant to show Him forth:

> I say, it's meant to hide Him all it can,
> And that's what all the blessed Evil's for.
> Its use in Time is to environ us,
> Our breath, our drop of dew, with shield enough
> Against that sight till we can bear its stress.
>
> *Robert Browning*

Only when the hearer assumes that what has happened may, even in changed circumstances, happen again and affect him, will he give an assent to the story with something amounting to faith.

Ulrich Simon

As Kirkegaard argued in his 'Sickness unto Death' the opposite of sin is not virtue but faith ... By faith here is not meant intellectual assent to a number of doctrinal propositions. It could be defined as self-confidence, except that, as we shall see, the self in which confidence is placed could be the limited superficial self, and this would make self-confidence the very opposite of faith. Perhaps therefore, a better definition would be confidence in life, the trustful attitude of a child belonging to a loving family. Faith is not a conviction since a conviction is the result of an intellectual process concerned with assessing evidence. Faith, on the other hand, is intuitive. It is a given (not acquired) certainty that the forces on our side are greater than the forces opposed to us. In Christian language, this is faith in God.

H. A. Williams

For William Temple our security is of faith won by personal loyalty. For Hans Küng what ultimately counts is trust (= faith in the New Testament). This personal loyalty, this trust, is of the essence of love.

Harry Williams defines faith as 'Confidence in life, the trustful attitude of a child belonging to a loving family'. In the family this confidence is given to us by our parents; it is they who mediate faith in God to us. Failing the family, that faith may be mediated through others who, often quite unconsciously, radiate it to those around them. Confidence in them, – in those who have confidence in life – communicates that same confidence to us. Such faith is not acquired intellectually, but intuitively, though reason has its part to play in distinguishing faith from credulity.

The Christian who is also in any degree a philosopher will not claim that by reason he can irrefragibly establish his faith; indeed, it is possible that his search may lead him to nothing but perplexity, from which he saves himself only by falling back on his unreasoned convictions, which come to him from the authority of the saints or from his own specifically religious experience.
William Temple

By faith Abraham, when he was called to go out into a place which he should after receive for an inheritance, obeyed; and he went out, not knowing whither he went . . . For he looked for a city which hath foundations, whose builder and maker is God.
Hebrews 11:8,10

Religion is the possibility of the removal of every ground of confidence except confidence in God alone . . .
Karl Barth

If the immense achievements of autonomous reason seem to have produced a world which is at best meaningless and at worst full of demons, then it could be that Polanyi is right, that we shall not find renewal within the framework of the assumptions which the Enlightenment held to be 'self-evident', that there is needed a radical conversion, a new starting point which begins as an act of trust in divine grace as something simply given to be received in faith and gratitude.
Lesslie Newbigin

Reason is an inadequate tool for the comprehension of ultimate reality, but it is the only tool we have for distinguishing faith from credulity, true religion from superstition, enthusiasm from fanaticism.
Louis Jacobs

All fanaticism is a strategy to prevent doubt from becoming conscious.
H.A. Williams

The welcome given by some people to fundamentalist religious creeds and hardline political views could be an indication that the cost of doubt is too great for them to pay.

Roy Niblett

> You call for faith:
> I show you doubt, to prove that faith exists.
> The more of doubt, the stronger faith, I say,
> If faith o'ercomes doubt.
>
> *Robert Browning*

We too often forget that Christian faith is a principle of questioning and struggle before it becomes a principle of certitude and of peace. One has to doubt and reject everything in order to believe firmly in Christ, and after one has begun to believe, one's faith itself must be tested and purified. Christianity is not a set of foregone conclusions. The Christian mind is a mind that risks intolerable purifications, and sometimes, indeed very often, the risk turns out to be too great to be tolerated.

Thomas Merton

The difference between the sceptic and the believer is the frequency of faith and not the certitude of position . . . Neither Exodus nor Easter wins out or is totally blotted out by Buchenwald, but we encounter both polar experiences. The life of faith is lived between them.

Martin Buber

Doubt has always been one of the principal ingredients of faith ever since it was discovered that faith is like walking through strange country on a dark night.

Neville Ward

One has to understand faith as eyes to see, a vision in the light (with the Fourth Gospel) and not a leap in the dark (with the Enlightenment) a recognition of the living God present and active in life . . . But I can only love a person, and a person I meet. So God can only communicate his personal self to us, to be adored and loved, in and through persons, in and through each other.

John Coventry

Thou waitest for the spark from heaven and we,
Light half-believers in our casual creeds
Who hesitate and falter life away,
And lose to-morrow the ground won to-day –
Ah, do not we, Wanderer, await it too?
Matthew Arnold

Most of us are 'half-believers' fearing the 'intolerable purification' to which firm faith must lead. But we too await the spark from heaven, undeserved though it may be.

Proposing to act as if 'I believe' is a proposition that deserves more consideration than it normally gets. 'It is my prerogative to decide to act decisively, it is not within my prerogative to decide to believe unreservedly,' writes Professor Baelz – hence the role within the Christian circle of half-belief – 'experiment with life in love'.
Believing in the Church

The test of a true faith is the extent to which its religion is secular.
John Oman

Johnston's central argument, following Bernard Lonergan, is that it is possible to distinguish in religious experience between a superstructure which he calls 'belief' and an infrastructure which he calls 'faith'. 'The superstructure is the outer word, the outer revelation, the word spoken in history and conditioned by culture. The infrastructure, on the other hand, is the interior word, the word spoken to the heart, the inner revelation.' It is an inner gift which at first is, so to speak, formless. It is present in the heart prior to any outer cultural formulation.
Kenneth Cracknell

He taught me what it
means to be radical:
that it has something
to do with being sure
of where faith is
   rooted
   and
   grounded
within experience,
so that you are free
to question everything
and not to fear
truth or reality.

Christopher Byers

It could be said that imagination can take us thus far, to the limits of the imaginable, and that it then must give way to faith which enables us to go forward into the unknown, the unimaginable.

Edward Robinson

When a soul holds on to God in trust, whether in seeking Him or contemplating Him, this is the highest worship it can bring.

Mother Julian of Norwich

Lord, I believe: help thou mine unbelief.

Mark 9:24

25

HUMILITY

Lord, I am not worthy that you should come under my roof, but speak the word only and my soul shall be healed.
Matthew 8:8

Of all things the beholding and loving of the Maker maketh the soul to seem less in his own sight, and most filleth him with reverent dread and true meekness: with plenty of charity to his even-Christians.
Mother Julian of Norwich

To be humble and docile, to know the need of help and ask for it, and then to make both the asking and the acting an offering of worship and of love: this is the essential element in christian virtue, because it is this that preserves in the strength of the grown man the heart of the child.
Gerald Vann

Temperateness has two aspects. First of all, it is what gives the quality of humility and reverence to our attitude to material things. It is what enables us to love things instead of grabbing and mauling and battening on them; it is what enables us to contemplate and not to devour.
Gerald Vann

The true follower of Jesus Christ (to-day) is neither an 'insider' nor an 'outsider' but one who humbly serves his Lord as he suffers outside the camp, bearing the reproach of all who are within.

The action of the Christian is sheer unholy worldliness, however much it may be dressed up in religious garb, unless it is covered with the holiness of Christ, and Christ is always found on this earth in the form of a servant.

Christians should be distinguishable in the general life of society in two ways. The first is by their sense of mission, that is their ability to perform their work in such a way that its relation to God's wider purpose for mankind as defined by Jesus Christ becomes clear and significant. The other is by their ministry, that is by their willing, joyful and self-forgetful service. It is service not primarily of the organised Church or the Christian cause as one particular worldly interest among others, but of their fellow-men through the work itself. Christian men should be eager to enable the university, the school, the government department, the factory and the sports club to fulfil their own function under God. They should not, under the guise of zeal for the Lord's house, greedily try to subsume these functions under that of the Church.

Daniel Jenkins

In many things we shall do well to follow Galileo's recommendation to his readers 'to pronounce that wise, ingenious and modest sentence, "I do not know."'

Charles Coulson

> Saviour, and can it be
> That thou shouldst dwell with me?
> From thy high and lofty throne,
> Throne of everlasting bliss,
> Will thy majesty stoop down
> To so mean a house as this?

Charles Wesley

Preoccupation with our spiritual progress is unhealthy, a sign of our false self. We must accept our failures, whether they be real or imagined, as opportunities for growth in knowledge of the truth that God, and God alone, is our rock, our refuge and our strength.

Gerard W. Hughes

There is a very high rung which only one man in a generation can reach: That of having learned all secret wisdom and then praying like a little child.

Rabbi Mendel of Rymanov

Truly, I say to you, unless you turn and become like children, you will never enter the kingdom of heaven.
Matthew 18:3

Though true humility is a sure sign of grace, there are grave dangers on the way there. True humility does not mean constantly thinking what a poor, miserable specimen of humanity you are. It means being free from thinking about yourself at all. If we have experienced only brief periods of self-forgetfulness, it may be in some kind of creative work like painting or writing, or in concern for someone we love, those brief periods give us a glimpse of what it would be like to be totally free from self-concern. Such a state is not achieved by frantic effort; it is a gift of grace, and the nearer we come to receiving it the less we shall be aware of it.

Three of our quotations refer to preserving in the adult the heart of the child 'to know the need of help and to ask for it'. This also makes us less inclined to judge our neighbour.

The touching, entrancing beauty of Christianity consists, as much as in anything else, in its freedom from all fastidiousness. A soul that is fastidious is as yet only hovering round the precincts of Christianity, but it has not entered its sanctuary, where heroism is always homely, where the best always acts as stimulus towards being (in a true sense) but one of the semi-articulate, bovine, childish, repulsively second-third-fourth rate crowd. When I told you of my choking emotion in reading that scene of Jesus, the Light of the World (that he is this is a historic fact), as a menial servant at the feet of those foolish little fishermen and tax-gatherers, what is it that moves me but just that huge life-and-love-bringing paradox, here in its fullest activity? The heathen philosophies, one and all, failed to get beyond fastidiousness; only Christianity – a deeply *costingly* realized Christianity – got beyond it.
Von Hügel

He hath shewed strength with his arm: he hath scattered the proud in the imagination of their hearts. He hath put down the mighty from their seat: and hath exalted the humble and meek.
The Magnificat

It is not hard to demonstrate that all the main threats confronting the world today, from atomic war and ecological disaster to social and civilisational catastrophe – by which I mean the widening gulf between rich and poor individuals and nations – have hidden within them just one root cause: the imperceptible transformation of what was originally a humble message into an arrogant one.

Arrogantly, Man started believing that, as the pinnacle and lord of creation, he had a total understanding of nature and could do what he liked with it.

Vaclav Havel

A man who does not know how to humble himself, who loses respect for the little ones out of noisy self-awareness, becomes himself inwardly small and impoverished. Often a man is afraid to give his fundamental attitude to life it's right name: humility.

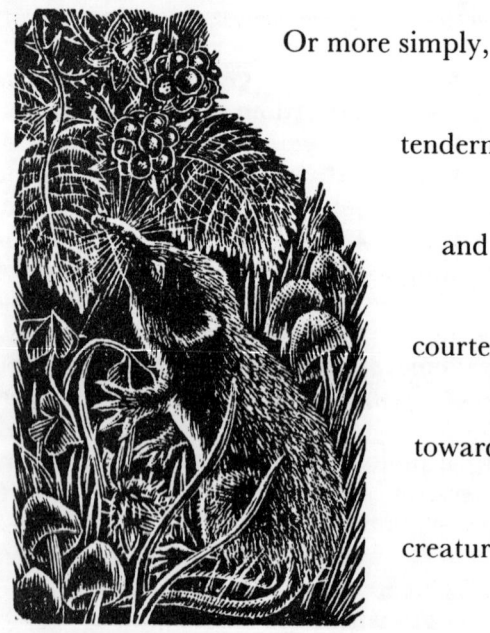

Or more simply,

tenderness

and

courtesy

towards

creatures.

Ladislaus Boros

He that is down needs fear no fall,
He that is low, no pride;
He that is humble ever shall
Have God to be his guide.

John Bunyan

26

OBEDIENCE

I saw that the carrying out of a vocation differed from the actions dictated by reason or inclination in that it was due to an impulse of an essentially and manifestly different order: and not to follow such an impulse when it made itself felt, even if it demanded impossibilities, seemed to me the greatest of all ills. Hence my conception of obedience.

Simone Weil

We can, I suppose, say that the sacrifice God wants is the offering of ourselves in obedience ... this, of course, goes beyond a willingness to do (or try to do) any specific deeds that God may require of us – important as that is. It is more than the acceptance of a set of rules or a programme of action. At its heart is an act of self-abandon to God which opens the way into newness of life, and which goes deeper than all moral outworkings. It is this act of self-abandon, by God's grace, that takes us into the feast of the Kingdom. It is the remedy for legalism. This is ... the answer to the age-long groping of the human race after the way to approach God and after the true meaning, the true nature, of sacrifice.

W. E. Prickett

Only he who believes is obedient, and only he who is obedient believes ... In the one case faith is the condition of obedience, and in the other obedience the condition of faith.

If we are to believe, we must obey a concrete command. Without this preliminary step of obedience, our faith will only be pious humbug, and lead us to the grace which is not costly. Everything depends on the first step. It has a unique quality of its own. The first step of obedience makes Peter leave his nets, and later get out of the ship; it calls upon the young man to leave his riches. Only this new existence, created through obedience, can make faith possible.

Dietrich Bonhoeffer

Our task is always the humble and courageous one of listening obediently and acting boldly.

Romano Guardini

Coming from noon-day rest on Vulture's Peak,
I saw an elephant, his bathing done,
Forth from the river issue. And a man,
Taking his goad, bade the great creature stretch
His foot: 'Give me thy foot.' The elephant
Obeyed, and to his neck the driver sprang.
I saw the untamed tamed, I saw him bent
To his master's will: and marking inwardly
I passed into the forest depths, and there
I' faith I trained and ordered all my heart.

Theragatha

The beginning is right reverence, not right resolve, because, above every other test of us, what we are able to honour is, in our deepest hearts, what we are, and, in our ultimate attainment, what we shall be . . . The order is first reverence, then surrender, then obedience, yet always one and indivisible, even when successive in their manifestation.

John Oman

There are all kinds of authority that society accustoms us to accept but in the last resort the only kind that really matters is that which we recognize in the person who has done, or known, or understood, something that we have not; has been somewhere that we have not . . . To recognise is to know from previous acquaintance. How come, then, that we recognise authority in *King Lear*, in *Cancer Ward*, in the Glagolitic Mass? Not because of any previous experience we have of ancient Britain, of the Soviet Camps, of Bohemian folk music, but because at a deeper level of our common humanity Shakespeare and Solzhenitsyn and Janaček all speak to us of something we already know, however dimly. Somewhere inside us an echo, a resonance is stirred; something in each of us says 'Yes'.

Edward Robinson

By thy leave, O Lord, from ore and mine, in furnace and foundry, with lathe and bore, we shape our tools and take our powers . . . Grant us, we pray thee, so to wield power as to learn reverence, so to take the force that we may bow to the mystery of nature, so to yield to thy authority that we rightly know our own.

Amen

What Simone Weil calls a 'vocation' – she does not confine the term to a career – has a distinctive quality all its own. But how to recognise such a call? Sometimes people speak too lightly of God telling them to do something, but the claim is not always convincing to others. Probably the real vocation is not one that we would easily talk about: it goes too deep for that. As a rule it will arise out of our circumstances or relations with other people, yet it will not be merely a matter of reasoning on the basis of those circumstances, and certainly not of mere inclination. Simone Weil speaks of following such an impulse even when it demands impossibilities. To say that this is most unreasonable would for most of us be the end of the argument, but on reflection we are bound to admit that the demands Jesus made on his disciples were indeed most unreasonable: to take no thought for the morrow, to turn the other cheek, to love their enemies, to be the servant of all, to leave their job and take up their cross – all quite unreasonable demands. This often leaves the would-be disciple in a state of confusion. How are we to know in practical terms where obedience lies? Dietrich Bonhoeffer tells us that everything depends upon the first step: obedience to a concrete demand. Once that step has been taken others will become clearer. We have entered upon 'a new existence', the life of faith, in which obedience constantly leads on to clearer vision, clearer intuitive understanding of 'vocation'.

It flashed upon her mind that the problem before her was essentially the same as that which had lain before Savonarola – the problem where the sacredness of obedience ended, and where the sacredness of rebellion began.

George Eliot

I have been struck by the insistence with which the Church constantly repeats this word: '*Christus factus est obediens usque ad mortem crucis*' (Christ became obedient unto death, even death on a cross Phil. 2:8) Clearly here is the precise and profound meaning of the cross: obedience, submission to the law of life. To work patiently until death, – and to accept everything, lovingly, including death itself: that is the essence of Christianity.

Teilhard de Chardin

... I think one must assert that Jesus could not be seen as God incarnate until he completed his obedience on the cross. Before then, he could be seen as chosen by God to be messiah and judge of all. But had he turned from the cross, he would have passed into history as yet another failed messiah, not as the triumphant Son of God.

Keith Ward

27

LOVE OF NEIGHBOUR

To love any one is nothing else than to wish that person good.
Thomas Aquinas

To love your neighbour as yourself means to aim at that for him at which you aim for yourself – namely, that he may love God with a perfect love. For you do not love him as yourself, unless you strive to draw him to that same Good as you are yourself pursuing.
Augustine of Hippo

There is no division of labour between love for one's own and love for strangers. On the contrary the condition for the existence of the former is the existence of the latter.
Erich Fromm

We usually assume that we begin by loving our own and hope that we shall gradually learn by extension to love strangers also, but Erich Fromm states that we cannot truly love our own unless we also love strangers. If the love is confined to our own family it will be possessive, whereas the love of strangers is disinterested. Once we have learned to love strangers, a disinterested love of our own family becomes possible.

Clever men are impressed with their difference from their fellowmen, but wise men are impressed with their solidarity.
R. H. Tawney

The way through to the vision of the Son of man and the knowledge of God, which is the heart of contemplative prayer, is by unconditional love of the neighbour, of 'the nearest Thou to hand'.
John A.T. Robinson

If I am afraid of my neighbour, I should realise that there is much in me of which I am afraid and of which he has every reason to be afraid. I am most clearsighted concerning those faults in him which need correcting in myself. I am dissatisfied with him when I am dissatisfied with myself. For it is equally true to say that I cannot love my neighbour until I love myself. When I feel frustrated, I shall judge him and condemn him for thoughts, words and deeds I felt compelled to inhibit. In fact I shall loathe my neighbour as myself. When I feel insignificant, the whole world will look insignificant to me, 'What a man sees in the world is only himself as he sees himself in the deep and honest privacy of his own heart'. My attitude to my neighbour reveals what I am.

Werner and Lotte Pelz

> I was angry with my friend;
> I told my wrath, my wrath did end.
> I was angry with my foe;
> I hid my wrath, my wrath did grow.
>
> *William Blake*

To love our neighbour in the fullest sense is simply to be capable of asking him: 'What is your torment?' It is to know that the unhappy person exists, not as one item in a collection, not as a sample of the social category labelled 'unhappy', but as a man, exactly like ourselves, who has once been marked in his own particular way by misfortune. For that the one thing needful is to know how to look upon him in a certain way.

This look is first of all an attentive look in which the soul empties herself of all precise content in order to receive into herself the being she is looking at just as he is, in all his truth. Only one who is capable of attention can do this.

Simone Weil

Only the wounded physician heals.

C. G. Jung

The direction of attention is, contrary to nature, outward, away from self which reduces all to a false unity, towards the great surprising variety of the world, and the ability so to direct attention is love.

One might at this point pause and consider the picture of human personality, or the soul, which has been emerging. It is in the capacity to love, that is to see, that the liberation of the soul from fantasy consists. The freedom which is a proper human goal is the freedom from fantasy, that is the realism of compassion . . . Freedom is not strictly the exercise of the will, but rather the experience of accurate vision which, when this becomes appropriate, occasions action. It is what lies behind and in between actions and prompts them that is important, and it is this area which should be purified. By the time the moment of choice has arrived the quality of attention has probably determined the nature of the act.
Iris Murdoch

Both Simone Weil and Iris Murdoch regard attention as the essence of love. Simone Weil writes here of attention to the other person as one who has been marked by misfortune; Iris Murdoch writes of attention away from self towards 'the great surprising variety of the world'. For Murdoch love is not primarily a matter of emotion, nor primarily a matter of the will, but a way of seeing. It is to be aware of the essence or potential of what one sees. It is the quality of attention, what we most attend to beforehand, which determines the way we will choose when the moment of choice arrives. To the question, 'why on earth did he decide to do that?' the answer must be, 'because he allowed the idea to occupy so much of his mind.'

What the mind keeps returning to in unguarded moments reveals the deeper feelings and motives which we are reluctant to admit even to ourselves.

When the service ends and the prayers have ceased, help me to bring their spirit into the world in which I live. May I love God above all, and my neighbour as myself, and be a living witness to the truth that never changes. Amen.
Forms of Prayer for Jewish Worship

Love of God is
the root,
love of our neighbour
the fruit
of the Tree of Life.
Neither can exist without
the other, but the one is
cause and the other effect.

William Temple

28

HUMAN LOVE/SPIRITUAL LOVE

For so long as the sexualized elements of the world had not reached the stage of personality, progeny alone could represent the reality in which the authors of generation in some way prolonged themselves. But as soon as love came into play, no longer only between parents but between two persons, the final goal necessarily appeared more or less indistinctly ahead of the lovers, the place at which not only their race but their personality would be at once preserved and completed . . . finally it is the total centre itself, much more than the child, that appears necessary for the consolidation of love. Love is a three term function: man, woman and God. Its whole perfection and success are bound up with the harmonious balance of these three elements.

Teilhard de Chardin

Let us love each other in the way that God wishes and let us not be frightened of the Love which is the very name of the Holy Ghost, and let us thus courageously await the will of Him who made us for His glory.

Leon Bloy
(Letter to his fiancée)

He (W. H. Vanstone) looks at behaviour which shows love to be inauthentic. Its falsity is shown first when any limit is set by the will of him who professes to love; secondly, by any attempt to control the one loved; and thirdly, by detachment. 'The lover gives to the object of his love a certain power over himself.'

From the three ways in which the falsity of love is expressed,

Vanstone determines three characteristics of authentic love as 'limitless, precarious and as vulnerable'.
Marcus Braybrooke

It is only when sex is understood as a symbol and preparation for the love of God that its true meaning can be seen. Because man is a spirit in a body of flesh, he has to learn to love through the flesh. But carnal love can never be more than a phase in human life and a preparation for love on a deeper level of being . . . This transformation of love from sexual into spiritual love, from Eros into Agape, is indeed the very purpose of life. It is a long, difficult and painful process; it involves a kind of crucifixion of our nature . . . this is the reason for all Christian asceticism.
Dom Bede Griffiths

Lovemaking ought to be as much an act of art as meditation as any other expression of 'whatever we want to express in its truest meaning' (Eckhart). It has every right to be as playful, as sensual, and as unitive as all our other mystical experiences.
Matthew Fox

The marriage relationship is not the antithesis of the God relationship; rather, as the Bible says, the one is the type of the other. (Eros) is not opposed to (agape) as something selfish and self-centred – even in its prototypal sexual form.

Yet the love of a woman and of God are not simply to be equated. When the two are set together, the former becomes utterly subordinate. Neither the fulfilment nor the demand is ultimately absolute – the claim of the finite Thou may not be averted by any other finite consideration, but beside the infinite it is nothing.
John A.T. Robinson

Within the spiritual community there is never, nor in any way, any immediate relationship of one to another, whereas human community expresses a profound, elemental human desire for community, for immediate contact with other human souls . . .

Human love is directed to the other person for his own sake, spiritual love loves him for Christ's sake. Therefore human love

seeks direct contact with the other person; it loves him not as a free person, but as one whom it binds to itself.
Dietrich Bonhoeffer

The mother's love is at first an absorbing delight, blunting all other sensibilities; it is an expansion of the animal existence; it enlarges the imagined range for self to move in: but in after years it can only continue to be joy on the same terms as other long-lived love – that is, by much suppression of self, and power of living in the experience of another.
George Eliot

I discovered in my own experience that spirituality without an earthly love for people can become the ultimate form of pride and a prison house for the human spirit, and that sexuality, unless it opens one's eyes to see the glory and to meet the reality in each other, can become the projection of our own deep-hidden needs onto other people and can destroy both us and them. Either one, split off from the other, can become diabolic.
Stephen Verney

There is a fundamental similarity of structure between love of God and love of a woman. This other, this 'Thou' can never be regarded as a 'piece' of my world, to be used for my own fruition and the fulfilment of my being. There is a severe limitation of the ego, resulting in the highest degree of unselfishness of which man is capable. The 'other' constitutes the sole end of my being, the sole spring of my action – which is pure listening.
John A.T. Robinson

We must all beware of reproaching those we love with want of confidence in us if they are not always ready to let us look into the corners of their hearts. Only those who respect the personality of others can be of real use to them.

I think, therefore, that no-one should compel himself to show to others more of his inner life than he feels it natural to show. We can do no more than let others judge for themselves what we inwardly and really are, and do the same ourselves with them.
Albert Schweitzer

Nothing is disastrous, except the loss of love.

Discovering a living relationship with God . . . contemplating him in the faces of others . . . restoring a human face to those disfigured . . . all of that is a single struggle, the struggle of love. Without love, what is the good of believing? Or of going so far as to give our bodies to the flames?

No, as we struggle nothing is really disastrous, except the loss of love.

Roger Schutz

To understand people and to hunt untiringly for matters to praise in them certainly cannot raise wrecks but they do far more to save human beings from drowning than the judgemental approach which costs nothing and is worth about as much. Hostility keeps us defensively locked in some obstinacy we are secretly sick of but cannot surrender until someone assures us that we are some good.

Neville Ward

To love somebody is not just a strong feeling – it is a decision, it is a judgement, it is a promise. If love were only a feeling, there would be no basis for the promise to love each other for ever. A feeling comes and it may go. How can I judge that it will stay for ever, when my act does not involve judgement and decision?

Erich Fromm

> Let me not to the marriage of true minds
> Admit impediments. Love is not love
> Which alters when it alteration finds,
> Or bends with the remover to remove:
> O, no! it is an ever-fixéd mark,
> That looks on tempests and is never shaken;
> It is the star to every wandering bark,
> Whose worth's unknown, although his height be taken.
> Love's not Time's fool, though rosy lips and cheeks
> Within his bending sickle's compass come;
> Love alters not with his brief hours and weeks,
> But bears it out even to the edge of doom.
> If this be error, and upon me prov'd,
> I never writ, nor no man ever lov'd.

William Shakespeare

None can be eternally united who have not died for each other.
Coventry Patmore

What are we to think about being 'in love'? Someone has described it as a form of mental illness which seriously clouds our judgement; the sooner we are cured of it the better. Teilhard de Chardin in his typically evolutionary way of thinking sees three stages in the 'evolution' of human love: 1) the pre-personal stage, for progeny alone 2) the personal stage – love between two persons, leading to 3) the final goal, personality preserved and completed in the 'total centre'. Love becomes a 'three term function' – man, woman and God.

Léon Bloy, writing to his fiancée, urges her not to be frightened of their love for each other, but to welcome it as a gift of God. For him there is no difference between being 'in love' and the gift of the Holy Ghost – provided they love each other 'in the way that God wishes'.

Bede Griffiths warns us of the cost of the transformation of sexual love into spiritual love. Although we learn to love through the flesh, that is only a preparation for love on a deeper level of being: to make carnal love the goal is to deny the very purpose of life.

Bonhoeffer sees human love as possessive – hence jealousy between lovers and crimes of passion: spiritual love does not seek direct contact with the other person, but loves him because God loves him or 'for Christ's sake'. Since the other person belongs not to us, but to God, we cannot bind him to ourself; he must be free to be servant of God.

For those contemplating marriage Erich Fromm's warning that love is more than strong feeling should make them pause before taking vows: 'it is a decision, it is a judgement, it is a promise'. Being 'in love', without decision, is the flimsiest basis for a life-long marriage: it is the marriage of Hollywood.

John Robinson seems to give the marriage relationship a more positive role as the 'type' of our relationship with God.

Many marriages are so short lived precisely because there is an intense desire for closeness and a minimal amount of space that allows free movement.
Henri Nouwen

Magnanimity lets the other be free, for that other must be great enough to be an image of God.
Ladislaus Boros

There is no surprise more magical than the surprise of being loved. It is the finger of God on a man's shoulder.
Charles Morgan

> The day will come when,
> after harnessing space,
>   the winds,
>   the tides,
>   and gravitation,
> we shall harness for God the energies of love.
> And on that day, for the second time
> in the history of the world,
>   we shall have discovered fire.
> *Teilhard De Chardin*

29

LOVE OF ENEMIES

You have heard that it was said, 'You shall love your neighbour and hate your enemy'. But I say to you, Love your enemies and pray for those who persecute you, so that you may be sons of your Father who is in heaven; for he makes his sun rise on the evil and on the good, and sends rain on the just and on the unjust.

Matthew 5. 43:45

The rule is that we should judge all men to be sinners but treat all men as born for eternity. We are to love all men in spite of the fact that they are sinners, partly because we know that we are sinners ourselves. We are to love them even when they go on sinning – for otherwise how could Christ have loved us? We are to love them even if we have to fight them – we have to love our enemies and never treat them as sub-human or as children of the devil, even if they treat others so; for otherwise how would mankind ever be lifted above barbarism? Much depends on what we are trying to do with the world and for the Christian it is not sufficient just to beat the sinner and conquer him or score over him – the object is to win him from his sins. Even if we have to fight him we do not give up that hope, do not even cease to be sorry for him somewhere or other – do not fight as the pagans do, with an idea that the sinners can be destroyed or that they can be rendered incapable of sinning any more. Therefore, let the non-Christians rise as hot and angry and Pharisaical as they like – which after all is the essence of much of our modern barbarism – but the Christian though he must be greatly distressed, has no right to be angry or surprised or Pharisaical when confronted by the spectacle of human wilfulness or even cruelty. The Christian understands it better than anyone else does – understands it as one who feels himself a partner in man's universal sin. For the Christians are not the righteous – they are the ones who confess themselves to be sinners. And they have a safety-valve against certain kinds of hardness of heart by that fact.

Herbert Butterfield

What does it really mean to be a Christian? What makes the Christian different from other men is the 'peculiar', the 'extraordinary', the 'unusual', that which is not a matter of course . . . It is the life described in the beatitudes, the life of the followers of Jesus, the light which lights the world, the city set on a hill, the way of self-renunciation, of utter love, of absolute purity, truthfulness and meekness. It is unreserved love for our enemies, for the unloving and the unloved, love for our religious, political and personal adversaries. In every case it is the love which was fulfilled in the cross of Christ . . . the cross is the differential of the Christian religion.

Dietrich Bonhoeffer

Love asks nothing in return, but seeks those who need it. And who needs our love more than those who are consumed with hatred and are utterly devoid of love? Who in other words deserves our love more than our enemy? Where is love more glorious and worthy to be praised than where she dwells in the midst of her enemies?

Dietrich Bonhoeffer

But Bonhoeffer, who wrote so movingly about love of enemies, was faced with a traumatic decision when he was challenged to support a plot to kill Hitler. He did support the plot almost at the risk of his own soul, certainly at the risk of his life.

There is a Japanese story of a Samurai (a member of the military caste) who wanted to avenge the murder of his father. When at last he found the murderer and drew his sword to kill him, the murderer spat in his face. This roused the anger of the Samurai – so that he sheathed his sword and walked away. Why? Because his anger had turned it into a personal act and that was not what he had come for.

Perhaps Bonhoeffer joined the plot to kill Hitler not because of any personal animosity, but because of the appalling suffering Hitler was causing for millions of others. As Marcus Braybrook writes in Time to

Meet 'there is a rabbinical saying, "Whoever is merciful to the cruel will end by being indifferent to the innocent". Perhaps here there may be a difference between our own feelings towards one who has injured us and our concern for others who have been injured and their proper demand for justice or redress.'

Respect and love ought to be extended also to those who think or act differently than we do in social, political, and religious matters, too. In fact, the more deeply we come to understand their ways of thinking through such courtesy and love, the more easily will we be able to enter into dialogue with them.

This love and good will, to be sure, must in no way render us indifferent to truth and goodness. Indeed love itself impels the disciples of Christ to speak the saving truth to all men. But it is necessary to distinguish between error, which always merits repudiation, and the person in error, who never loses the dignity of being a person, even when he is flawed by false or inadequate religious notions. God alone is the judge and searcher of hearts; for that reason He forbids us to make judgments about the internal guilt of anyone.

The teaching of Christ even requires that we forgive injuries, and extends the law of love to include every enemy.

Vatican II
The Church in the Modern World

I offer up unto Thee my prayers and intercessions, for those especially who have in any matter hurt, grieved, or found fault with me, or who have done me any damage or displeasure.

For all those also whom, at any time, I have vexed, troubled, burdened, and scandalised, by words or deeds, knowingly or in ignorance: that Thou wouldst grant us all equally pardon for our sins, and for our offences against each other.

Thomas à Kempis

Almighty God, have mercy upon – and – and on all that bear me evil will and would me harm; and their faults and mine together, by such easy, tender, merciful means as Thine infinite wisdom best can divine, vouchsafe to amend and redress, and make us saved souls in heaven together with Thee and Thy blessed saints, O glorous Trinity, for the bitter passion of our sweet Saviour Christ. Amen

Sir Thomas More

> There is neither enemy nor alien
> nor even a stranger. I have indeed
> befriended all.
>
> *Sikh Prayer*

One afternoon, as he sat in a department store autographing copies, a well-dressed but deranged woman stabbed him in the chest near the heart. As soon as King recovered consciousness, he asked about his assailant, saying urgently, 'She needs help. She is not responsible for the violence she has done to me. Don't punish her; don't prosecute her; get her healed.'

Mary Craig on Martin Luther King

Peace is something you make with your enemies, not with your bosom friends.

Amos Oz

O Lord, remember not only the men and women of good will, but also those of ill will. But do not remember all the suffering they have inflicted on us: remember the fruits we have bought, thanks to this suffering – our comradeship, our loyalty, our humility, our courage, our generosity, the greatness of heart which has grown out of all this, and when they come to judgement let all the fruits which we have borne be their forgiveness.

Prayer written by an unknown prisoner in Ravensbruck concentration camp and left by the body of a dead child

The Parable of the Saw
The Blessed One said: 'Though robbers or highwaymen might carve you limb from limb with a double-handed saw, yet even then whoever gives way to hatred is not a follower of my teaching. You should train yourselves like this: "Our minds will not become deranged, we will not utter evil speech, we will remain with a friendly heart, devoid of hatred: and, beginning with these people, we will develop the thought of loving-kindness."'

Reflections on the Parable of the Saw
The Blessed One said: 'There are five ways of speaking which others might use in addressing you. They might speak at a right time, or at a wrong time; according to fact, or not according to fact; gently or harshly; on what is connected with the goal, or on what is not connected with the goal; with a mind of friendliness, or with a mind full of hatred.
But if you were to reflect repeatedly on the parable of the saw, would you see any way of speech, subtle or gross, that you could not endure?
Majjhima Nikaya

An eye for an eye – that way the whole world will become blind.
Albert Einstein

The teaching of Jesus that we should love our enemies was perhaps the most revolutionary of all his teachings. After two thousand years Christians are still sharply divided in their interpretation of it. Some say that it applies only to relationships between individuals; it was never intended to apply to international relations. So there are Christians who support the nuclear deterrent and would apparently be prepared to press the button to kill many millions indiscriminantly in retaliation for a nuclear attack. Others, like the Quakers, believe that Christian discipleship implies a refusal to retaliate in all circumstances, and therefore implies pacifism and the use of non-violent methods to contain violence. Dietrich Bonnhoeffer, who wrote so movingly about love of enemies, in the end joined in a plot to kill Hitler. Perhaps he could do that without hatred? In the New Testament the early church seems to make an exception of Judas Iscariot. In doing so did they truly interpret the mind of Christ? In Matthew 26:50 Jesus addresses Judas as a "friend" at the moment of his betrayal. Perhaps different views are already reflected in the Gospels.

Father, forgive them; for they know not what they do.
Luke 23:34

30

JOY

I will go unto the altar of God, to God who giveth joy to my youth.
Psalm 43:4

Rav said: A man will have to give account in the judgement day of every good thing which he might have enjoyed and did not.
Yerushalmi

This is the true joy of life, the being used for a purpose recognised by yourself as a mighty one.
Bernard Shaw

The commands of God are all designed to make us more happy than we can possibly be without them.
Thomas Wilson

'Joy' for the Wesleys, was not primarily an attribute of man's at all, but of God's – and in particular, of God in Creation. Joy was thought of as the divine concomitant of creativity. Man's joy came from sharing in the joy of his Master. In this man was only echoing the entire cosmos. At the Creation 'the morning stars sang together, and all the sons of God shouted for joy.'
Stephen Prickett

> Man was made for Joy and Woe;
> And when this we rightly know,
> Thro' the World we safely go,
> Joy and woe are woven fine,
> A clothing for the soul divine.
> *William Blake*

'Joy and woe are woven fine'. In the great prophets of Israel, in Jesus, in the Saints, joy and suffering are an integral part of the fabric of their lives, so that we cannot begin to understand the meaning of the one without the other. The writer of the letter to the Hebrews says of Jesus that *'for the joy that was set before him he endured the Cross'*. We usually contrast joy and suffering; Blake saw that they were *'woven fine'*. Paul wrote to the Corinthians, *'in our sorrows we have always cause for joy'* (2 Cor. 6:10). After being flogged *'the apostles went out from the Council rejoicing that they had been found worthy to suffer indignity for the sake of the Name'* (Acts 5:41) *This is a mystery discovered only in obedience.*
Even the artist's joy in creation is not unmixed with suffering. It involves (as Iris Murdoch insists) a kind of death to self. So to share in the creative joy of the Creator is to die to self and live to God through *'the love of many things'* (Vincent Van Gogh.)

> He who binds to himself a Joy
> Doth the winged life destroy;
> But he who kisses the Joy as it flies
> Lives in Eternity's sunrise.
>
> *William Blake*

For him (Luke) the gospel of Jesus is something joyful and new, especially for the lowly – in word and deed – a joyful new thing bringing radical change and renewal. Luke is fond of seeing joy in many events of Jesus' life. For him the announcement of the birth of Jesus is already good tidings. Grace is the forgiveness of sins; therefore there is joy over every sinner who repents; grace is the resurrection of Jesus, so there is joy at this event.

Edward Schillebeeckx

Behold, I bring you good tidings of great joy.

Luke 2.10

Joy is everywhere: it is in the earth's green covering of grass: in the blue serenity of the sky: in the reckless exuberance of spring: in the severe abstinence of grey winter: in the living flesh that animates our bodily frame: in the perfect poise of the human figure, noble and upright: in living, in the exercise of all our powers: in the acquisition of knowledge: in fighting evils: in dying for gains we never can share. Joy is there everywhere.

Rabindranath Tagore

> Shout to the Lord all the earth,
> serve the Lord with joy,
> come before Him with singing.
>
> *Psalm 100:1–2*

Break forth into joy, sing together, ye waste places of Jerusalem: for the Lord hath comforted his people, he hath redeemed Jerusalem.

Is. 52:9

> Without arms or charm of culture,
> Unimportant persons
> From an unimportant Province,
> They did as the Spirit bid,
> Went forth into a joyless world
> Of swords and rhetoric
> To bring it joy.
>
> *W. H. Auden*

Wherefore seeing we also are compassed about with so great a cloud of witnesses, let us lay aside every weight, and the sin which doth so easily beset us, and let us run with patience the race that is set before us, looking unto Jesus the author and finisher of our faith: who for the joy that was set before him endured the cross, despising the shame, and is set down at the right hand of God.

Hebrews 12:1

> Happy are those who live in Your house
>   and can always praise You.
> Happy the pilgrim inspired by You,
>   they journey to You in their heart.
> They pass through the dry sad valley
>   and make it seem a place of springs,
>   as if the early rain covered it with blessings.
> They go from strength to strength
>   to appear before God in Zion
>
> *Psalm 84*
> *vv. 4–7*

The harvest of the Spirit is love, joy, peace, good temper, gentleness, goodness, humility and self-control.
Galatians 5:22

Take your longing, your prayer, your love and throw all that in the scale of life and joy! Of all the stupidities with which the devil surrounds us one is the most destructive: 'Life is boring'. The soul of man is created for divine joy.
Ladislaus Boros

True happiness and spiritual joy does not mean living on a perpetual 'high', but may be compared to the ballast in a ship. With ballast the ship will roll in a storm, just as a person capable of true happiness and joy will feel pain in a crisis, but the storm will not capsize the boat which will quickly right itself, even when struck by a wave. Similarly, true happiness and spiritual joy does not mean living on a continuous high, unaffected by grief, sadness or loss, the pain of others, but it does mean that we shall not sink into despair under the blows, but will recover peace and tranquility when the storm is over.
Gerard W. Hughes

> Nothing is so beautiful as spring –
>   When weeds, in wheels, shoot long and lovely and lush;
>   Thrush's eggs look little low heavens, and thrush
> Through the echoing timber does so rinse and wring
> The ear, it strikes like lightnings to hear him sing;
>   The glassy peartree leaves and blooms, they brush
>   The descending blue; that blue is all in a rush
> With richness; the racing lambs too have fair their fling.

What is all this juice and all this joy?
   A strain of the earth's sweet being in the beginning
In Eden garden. – Have, get, before it cloy,
   Before it cloud, Christ, lord, and sour with sinning,
Innocent mind and Mayday in girl and boy,
   Most, O maid's child, thy choice and worthy the winning.
Gerard Manley Hopkins

I that so long
Was Nothing from Eternitie,
Did little think Joys as Ear or Tongue,
To Celebrate or See:
Such Sounds to hear, such Hands to feel, such Feet,
Beneath the Skies, on such a Ground to meet.
Thomas Traherne

The God who is set up against the Creation and who is somehow jealous of his own work is, to my mind, nothing but an idol.
Gabriel Marcel

Give me my scallop-shell of quiet,
My staff of faith to walk upon,
My scrip of joy, immortal diet,
My bottle of salvation,
My gown of glory, hope's true gage,
And thus I'll take my pilgrimage.
Sir Walter Ralegh

Give goodness its reward
Give journey safe through death
Give joy that has no end.
13th century hymn

31

WORLD PEACE – RECONCILIATION

For the Kingdom of God is justice . . . peace and joy, inspired by the Holy Spirit.
Romans 14:17

Aim at peace with all men . . . for without that no-one will see the Lord.
Hebrews 12:14

For he is himself our peace. Gentiles and Jews, he has made the two one, and in his own body of flesh and blood has broken down the enmity which stood like a dividing wall between them.
Ephesians 2:14

Gentleness and pity when not regulated by reason and dictated by love, can deform human nature as much as violence, since they are then manifestations of cowardice, not of charity.
Jacques Maritain

The nations themselves need some Society that may include themselves, whose basis shall be a common purpose, not springing from merely individual interest and a preference for fellowship, as against the horrors of war, but arising out of loyalty to an all inclusive Kingdom and a common Master, and expressing itself in common action in service of that Master and Kingdom.
William Temple

Everyone is engaged in the frantic pursuit of 'security', and imagines that this is to be achieved by keeping potential enemies in subjection.
Bertrand Russell

But nothing is accomplished by an attempt to make a portion of mankind secure at the expense of another portion, – Frenchmen at the expense of Germans, capitalists at the expense of wage earners, white men at the expense of yellow and so on. Such methods only increase terror in the dominant group, lest just resentment should lead the oppressed to rebel. Only 'justice' can give security: and by 'justice' I mean the recognition of the equal claims of all human beings.
Bertrand Russell

The rule of God (the word itself sounds theocratic) is the disarming appearance in the world of the love of God in the form of human, peace-making love which does not dominate but which liberates and serves, which provides critical prophetic opposition, that is, active opposition, to everything that makes universal shalom impossible, in the world and in the churches.
Edward Schillebeeckx

The peace of this world is always uncertain, unless men keep the peace of God. And war among men defiles this world, but death in the Lord renews it.
T. S. Eliot

I will explain to them (the French workers) that we can no longer use the old weapons. We must constantly be inventing new methods of action which will not end in destruction.
Lech Walesa, replying to a French journalist on his arrival in Paris in September 1981

This question of the strong and the weak touches the whole problem of our society, and, in the last analysis of war and peace as well. . . . If weakness leads to a sense of failure, strength too has its vicious circle: one must go on being stronger and stronger for fear of suffering an even more crushing defeat, and this race in strength leads humanity inevitably to general collapse.
Paul Tournier

Our Father God, you who are not bound by the same fears as we are, you who see things as they really are, may your voice be heard and believed. May your will be done on Earth as in Heaven, that people may live in trust and peace.

Give us what we need for this day: food and hope, a meaning to our lives, a belief that the child born to-day will live to grow old.

Forgive us where we have added to hate, added to distrust, colluded in the creation of weapons of fear, as we forgive those who have done us harm.

Deliver us from the temptation of thinking that your new earth will come through a nuclear war, or that somehow people will survive, or that we need to do nothing.

And deliver us from the evil of believing that there is good in weapons that can destroy all human life.

For it is your way of sharing that we would follow, your power in trusting that we would take, your light of truth and joy that we would show the world. May it be so. Amen.

A paraphrase of the Lord's prayer
The Church of Scotland

Peace is not the product of terror or fear.
Peace is not the silence of cemeteries.
Peace is not the silent result of violent repression.
Peace is the generous, tranquil contribution of all to the good of all.
Peace is dynamism. Peace is generosity.
It is right and it is duty. In it each one feels at home
in this beautiful family that the Epiphany brightens with God's light.

Oscar Romero

Your first aim here on earth should be to be at peace with all men, Jew and non-Jew alike. Contend with no-one. Your home should be a place of quietness and happiness, where no harsh word is ever heard, but love, friendship, modesty, and a spirit of gentleness and reverence rules all the time. But this spirit must not end with the home. In your dealings with the world you must allow neither money nor ambition to disturb you. Forgo your rights in matters of honour, if need be, and above all envy no man. For the main thing is peace, peace with the whole world.

Rabbi Joel ben Abraham Shemariah

How can love be expressed between nations? Clearly we are here dealing with something quite different from individual personal relationships. Collectives of tens of millions are never all of one mind, with a readiness to forgive, turn the other cheek, renounce the use of force to compel and to control weaker nations. The demands Jesus made of his disciples often seem idealistic and even irrelevant when applied to nations. In considering this problem William Temple gave the definitive answer: what the Christian citizen has to do in most of his problems concerning the relations of corporate groups is 'to dedicate himself in the power of love to the establishment of justice'.

Grant us the benediction of the peacemakers in the things of reconciliation that force and state cannot attain. Give us endurance, not grim and hard, but gentle and joyous in the peace of thy eternity. Show us the long-suffering that is more strong than anger, more ultimate than hate.
Kenneth Cragg

Peace is not the absence of tension but the presence of justice.
Martin Luther King

Lord of the world, grant us wonder, give us reverence, subdue us to courtesy, guide us to unity, school us to gratitude.
Let us know our mastery to be of thy mercy. Let thy peace rule, in the great and in the small.

> Give us peace with thee,
> Peace with men, peace with ourselves,
> And free us from all fear.
> *Dag Hammarskjold*

Lead me from the unreal, the untruth to truth.
Lead me from the darkness to light, from ignorance to knowledge.
Lead me from death to immortality.
Let peace prevail everywhere.
Let peace fill our heart, our world, our universe.

OM . . . May divine blessing shower upon us. May peace pervade the whole human race. May there be an abundance of plants that we use. May humanity prosper, O God, and animals flourish.
OM . . . . PEACE . . . .

| Shantih | Shantih | Shantih |
| Peace | Peace | Peace |

Hindu Prayers

V
SELF OFFERING

32

FRIENDSHIP

He truly loves a friend who loves God in the friend, either because God is in him or that He may be in him.
Augustine of Hippo

Blessed is the man that loves thee, O God, and his friend in thee, and his enemy for thee. For he alone loses no-one that is dear to him, if all are dear in God, who is never lost.
Augustine of Hippo

What is meant by trust? . . . I think that trust has to do with granting someone else a prior claim on our life and action: we open ourselves out to the other person and up to a point place ourselves at his disposal, without being absolutely sure of the trustworthiness of the other. Trust means surrendering oneself to another without an ultimate reinsurance.
Karl Rahner

A friendship is spoiled as soon as coercion, if only for a moment, takes precedence over the desire to preserve in each partner the option of free consent. In all human affairs, coercion is the principle of impurity. Any friendship is impure if it contains even a trace of the wish to please or displease. In a perfect friendship these two desires are totally absent. The two friends fully accept that they are two and not one: they respect the distance which the fact of being distinct creatures puts between them. It is only with God that a human being may rightly wish to be directly united.
Simone Weil

No trace of a desire to please between friends? That seems at first sight nonsense. But Simone Weil does not write nonsense. What does she mean? Perhaps the clue is to be found in the fact that the friends are 'distinct creatures'. Each has unique inborn gifts. The ultimate betrayal is to fail to become ourselves, and the danger of a possessive type of friendship is that in trying to please our friend we cease to be ourself.

Friendship is a disinterested commerce between equals; love, an abject intercourse between tyrants and slaves.
Oliver Goldsmith

If a man does not make new acquaintance as he advances through life, he will soon find himself left alone. A man, Sir, should keep his friendship in constant repair.
Samuel Johnson

The greater the friendship the more permanent it should be. The greatest friendship is that between man and wife, who are coupled not only by physical intercourse, which even among animals conduces to a certain sweet friendship, but also for the sharing of domestic life.
St Thomas Aquinas

> When to the sessions of sweet silent thought
> I summon up remembrance of things past,
> I sigh the lack of many a thing I sought,
> And with old woes new wail my dear times' waste:
> Then can I drown an eye, unus'd to flow,
> For precious friends hid in death's dateless night,
> And weep afresh love's long since cancell'd woe,
> And moan the expense of many a vanish'd sight:
> Then can I grieve at grievances foregone,
> And heavily from woe to woe tell o'er
> The sad account of fore-bemoaned moan,
> Which I new pay as if not paid before.
>   But if the while I think on thee, dear friend,
>   All losses are restor'd and sorrows end.
> *William Shakespeare*

Friendship cannot exist without forgiveness of sins continually.
William Blake

For it is not an open enemy, that hath done me this dishonour: for then I could have borne it.
Neither was it mine adversary, that did magnify himself against me: for then peradventure I would have hid myself from him.
But it was even thou, my companion: my guide, and mine own familiar friend.
We took sweet counsel together: and walked in the house of God
as friends.

Psalm 55: 12–15

To forgive enemies (Hayley) – does pretend,
Who never in his life forgave a friend.

William Blake

Freeze, freeze, thou bitter sky,
That dost not bite so nigh
   As benefits forgot:
Though thou the waters warp,
Thy sting is not so sharp
   As friend remember'd not.

William Shakespeare

True happiness
Consists not in the multitude of friends,
But in the worth and choice.

Ben Jonson

The more the separateness and differentness of other people is realized, and the fact seen that another man has needs and wishes as demanding as one's own, the harder it becomes to treat a person as a thing.

Iris Murdoch

That fellowship of love is the end for which we were created and for which our nature as God fashioned it is designed.

William Temple

There are three sights which warm my heart
and are beautiful in the eyes of the Lord and of men:
concord among brothers, friendship among neighbours,
and a man and wife who are inseparable.
Ecclus 25:1

Each of us carries the imprint
of the friend met along the way;
In each the trace of each.
For good or evil
In wisdom or in folly
Each stamped by each.
Primo Levi

When I can no longer bear my loneliness I take it to my friends. For I must share it with all the friends of God. 'Do you suffer?' 'So do I!'
Mechtild of Magdeburg

Think where man's glory most begins and ends,
And say my glory was I had such friends.
W. B. Yeats

No longer do I call you servants, for the servant does not know what his master is doing; but I have called you friends, for all that I have heard from my Father I have made known to you.
John 15:15

Greater love hath no man than this, that a man lay down his life for his friends.
John 15:13

33

GENEROSITY

Each one must do as he has made up his mind, not reluctantly or under compulsion, for God loves a cheerful giver.
2 Corinthians 9:7

In all things I have shown you that by so toiling one must help the weak, remembering the words of the Lord Jesus, how he said, 'It is more blessed to give than to receive'.
Acts 20:35

There are eight degrees in the giving of charity, one higher than the other:

> He who gives grudgingly, reluctantly, or with regret.
> He who gives less than he should, but gives graciously.
> He who gives what he should, but only after he is asked.
> He who gives before he is asked.
> He who gives without knowing to whom he gives, although the recipient knows the identity of the donor.
> He who gives without making his identity known.
> He who gives without knowing to whom he gives, and the recipient not knowing from whom he receives.
> He who helps a fellowman to support himself by a gift, or a loan, or by finding employment for him, thus helping him to become self-supporting.

Maimonides

A man may give liberally, and yet because he gives unlovingly and wounds the heart of the poor, his gift is in vain, for it has lost the attribute of charity; a man may give little, but because his heart goes with it his deed and himself are blessed.
Baba Batra

Give to him who begs from you, and do not refuse him who would borrow from you.

Matthew 5:42

Give, and it will be given to you; good measure, pressed down, shaken together, running over, will be put into your lap. For the measure you give will be the measure you get back.

Luke 6:38

Earn all you can, save all you can, give all you can.

John Wesley

There are two ways of giving things. They may be given as a sign or symbol of the giving of oneself, or they may be given as a substitute for the giving of oneself.

G. A. Lyward

All of us are challenged by the necessity of sharing. This cannot be limited to a restricted area, to one local or national community. In the renewed awareness of the needs of people throughout the world, Christians will be required more and more to see themselves as part of all humanity. That is our vocation to catholicity, to universality.

Roger Schutz

Let our superfluities give way to our neighbour's conveniences: our conveniences to our neighbour's necessities: our necessities to his extremities.

John Wesley

Once he was standing opposite the temple treasury, watching as people dropped their money into the chest. Many rich people were giving large sums. Presently there came a poor widow who dropped in two tiny coins, together worth a farthing. He called his disciples to him. 'I tell you this,' he said: 'this poor widow has given more than any of the others; for those others who have given had more than enough, but she, with less than enough, has given all that she had to live on.'

Mark 12:41–44

As thy substance is, give alms of it according to thine abundance: if thou have little, be not afraid to give alms according to that little.

Tobit 4:8

There is a recklessness in the teaching of Jesus which frankly does not appeal to the modern middle-class Christian, so concerned about security. It is legitimate to ask whether a family man would have spoken or acted so recklessly. Reason suggests that we should aim at 'a right balance,' but Jesus does not appear to leave room for that kind of calculation. It is a challenge we cannot avoid that is finely expressed by Gerard Hughes:

In the parable of the Two Sons, the Father is represented as foolishly lavish toward the prodigal son, even more prodigal than the boy! He would have shown admirable generosity if he had accepted his son home again after disgracing the family; to watch for the son's return, to rush out as soon as he comes in sight, to embrace, clothe with sandals, a cloak, a ring and then to kill the prize calf and throw a party is all a bit excessive, and our prudent, measured and well-controlled selves, brought-up on Aristotle's 'virtue lies in the mean between extremes', can have every sympathy with the sober-minded, hard-working elder brother. Faced with his elder son's indignation, the Father remains his lavish self, telling him 'all I have is yours'.

The Father is also represented as financially imprudent, forgiving the debtor who owes ten thousand talents, a fortune of many millions of pounds in our terms, without a qualm, but getting into a rage with that same debtor when he tried to squeeze a paltry sum from someone else. The wrath of the Father is reserved for the mean and stingy, like this extortionate debtor, or like Dives who feasts richly while Lazarus starves at his gate ... The Father is pictured as so careless about money that ... he pays last-minute workers as much as full-day workers and seems opposed to prudence in money matters. The careful steward who kept his talent safe and intact for his master's return is condemned: the other two stewards who took risks and produced more talents are praised.

Gerard W. Hughes

As Abraham was sitting at the opening of his tent in the heat of the day, he loooked up and saw three men standing in front of him. When he saw them, he ran from the opening of his tent to meet them and bowed low to the ground. 'Sirs' he said, 'if I have deserved your favour, do not pass by my humble self without a visit. Let me send for some water so that you may wash your feet and rest under a tree; and let me fetch a little food so that you may refresh yourselves. Afterwards you may continue the journey which has brought you my way.'
Genesis 18: 1–5

Do not neglect to show hospitality to strangers, for thereby some have entertained angels unawares.
Hebrews 13:2

34

GRATITUDE

What is gladness without gratitude
And where is gratitude without a God?

Coventry Patmore

Not perhaps the God of the philosophers, but certainly the God of every human being as a human being. Just before writing this I heard of a mother whose brilliant son had developed a terminal illness. She had just been informed by a specialist that recent tests showed that all sign of the illness had disappeared; he was completely cured. What are the first words any mother would say in such circumstances: 'Oh, Thank God!'

The Christian is one who has forever given up the hope of being able to think of himself as a good man . . . In a sense we can say that he has given up the effort to be good. That is no longer his aim. He is seeking to do one thing and one thing only – to pay back something of the unpayable debt of gratitude to Christ who loved him as a sinner and gave Himself for him. And in this new and self-forgetting quest he finds that which – when he sought it directly – was forever bound to elude him, the good life.

Lesslie Newbigin

In Islam, also, gratitude is of the essence of belief:

The nature of theism is the perspective of gratitude. Reverently responding to experience is, for the Qur'an, the temper of belief.

Kenneth Cragg

But gratitude has far wider implications:

'Augustine . . . was not likely to underestimate the power, of envy in determining the relations of the "city" of the fallen with the "City" of God.

The "lust to dominate" is an equally potent force among the fallen beings. . .

But above all, there is pride: an omnipotent denial of dependence characterizes the attitude of the "earthly city" to the quite genuine values its members had created: its heroisms, its culture, its periods of peace. Throughout the *City of God*, it is to this basic denial of dependence, and so of gratitude, that Augustine will point, in politics, in thought, in religion.'

Peter Brown

Self-assertion can be understood as guilt only if it can be understood as ingratitude.

R. Bultman

> What can I return to the Lord
>   for all His generosity to me?
> I will lift up the cup of salvation
>   and call on the name of the Lord
> I will fulfil my promises to the Lord
>   in the presence of all His people.
>
> Precious in the sight of the Lord
>   are those who die, devoted to Him.
> I am Your servant, Lord, Your servant,
>   the child of a woman who served You.
> You freed me from my bonds
> To You I offer the offering of gratitude
>   and call on the name of the Lord.

Psalm 116

There is a very close relationship between charism (gift) and human talent. Talent is grace. One may be responsible or irresponsible for a talent that has been given (Matt. 25:14ff.) The talent put to good use humanizes if it is continually lived in a spirit of gratitude.

Leonardo Boff

Gratitude is of the essence of religion and ingratitude of the essence of sin. This is more easily understood by those of us who know that we have so much to be grateful for – a good home with loving parents, educational opportunities denied to many others, friends in whom the love of God has been manifest. But can we talk about gratitude to those who have never known a loving home, who, though naturally able, have been denied opportunities to develop their ability, whose environment has been one of crude materialism? Certainly the privileged have no right to preach to them, only to be alongside them where they are able to do so without condescension. Yet there are many who rise above circumstances. Where that occurs and grace and gratitude supervene over bitterness, we find qualities which often go far beyond the more facile achievements of the privileged.

> Sleep; and if life was bitter to thee, pardon,
>   If sweet, give thanks; thou hast no more to live;
>   And to give thanks is good, and to forgive.
>   *Algernon Charles Swinburne*

> Not when the sense is dim,
>   But now from the heart of joy,
> I would remember Him:
>   Take the thanks of a boy.
>   *H.C. Beeching*

O come, let us sing unto the Lord: let us heartily rejoice in the strength of our salvation.
Let us come before his presence with thanksgiving: and shew ourselves glad in him with psalms.
                        Psalm 95:1

If the only prayer you say in your whole life is Thank You, that will suffice.
                        Meister Eckhart

35

RISK

Mr and Mrs Alan Weaver went home to an empty flat last night after ignoring cynics who scoffed at their novel plan to raise funds for Bangladesh relief. In just over an hour nearly everything they had bought for their home since they married two years ago was auctioned in Shrewsbury town square.

All that is left in the couple's rented flat in Underdale Road, Shrewsbury, is a double bed, a carpet, which could not be lifted because it was stuck to the floor, a few cooking utensils and a cup and saucer and plate each.

The Times. January 31st 1975

Because human existence is always in movement and in a process of becoming, its decisive expression can take place only through an act which is more like a 'leap' than a gradual transition from one stage to another . . .

The meaning of this leap into the unknown is determined by the nature of the act rather than by its object; the experience of freedom is more fundamental than its particular mode of expression. In making a choice, says Kierkegaard, 'it is not so much a question of choosing the right as of the energy, the earnestness, the pathos with which one chooses' . . .

Ronald Grimsley on Kierkegaard

It is easy to live superficially and never to take the risk of diving into the depths and facing the terrors of the deep. The result is, living superficially, we are unable to reach out to God – because God is deep.

And at the same time we prove unable to reach out to our neighbour; because our neighbour can only meet us in the depths. On the surface he can only conflict with us.

Metropolitan Anthony Bloom

The risk of love is often feared, and sometimes altogether avoided, because it involves leaving ourselves open to the hurtfulness of being rejected. The commitment of love always implies acceptance of our vulnerability.

The New Testament understands sin as unbelief – not as immorality – as our inability to believe in our opportunities. We are sinners, not because we do this or leave that undone, but because we refuse to follow our hope, to trust our desires, to obey our vision; because we prefer to unlive our lives and cannot help fearing that to live them involves too much of a risk; because we feel secure only in doing that which denies the possibility of growth.

Werner & Lotte Pelz

No-one is built naturally for the radicalism of the Gospel. Yet it is through giving himself globally that a person grows. If he risks his whole life, that becomes the preparation for events beyond his wildest hopes. Situations of standstill, discouragement, or fierce struggle, far from demolishing, build him up. The moment comes when we receive what we no longer expected. What we had never dared to hope for arises: A gleam of Christ in us.

Roger Schutz

I want to assure you–
and I ask for your prayers to be faithful to this promise–
that I will not abandon my people
but that together with them I will run all the risks
that my ministry demands.

Oscar Romero

The leap of faith. All the demands Jesus made of his disciples involved quite unreasonable risks: To take no thought for the morrow, to return good for evil, to turn the other cheek, to love their enemies, to be the servant of all, to leave their job and to take up their cross and follow him. These are demands which nobody whose actions were determined solely by reason would be likely to accept; they all involve a leap of faith, becoming vulnerable, risking one's life. They involve a reversal of the mad search for security – through possessions, through nuclear weapons, through insurance policies. But only those who are secure are free to take risks – and where does our deepest security lie? Jesus said that anyone who took the big risk for his sake – through faith in him and his Way of forgiveness, service and love – would find his true self.

A sage took his disciples to the marketplace, so that they could watch a rope dancer risk his life. 'What are we supposed to learn from this?' they asked. The teacher answered: 'I also do not know why this man risks his life. But I am quite sure that while he is walking on the rope he is at peace within himself. And he is not thinking for a moment of the fact that he is earning a hundred gulden for what he is doing. If he did – he would surely fall!'

Antoine de St. Exupéry reflects on his experience of a forced landing of his mail plane in the Sahara:

Only when linked with our brothers by a common aim outside ourselves do we breathe freely, and the experience shows us that loving is not to look at each other but to look together in the same direction. Real friends are found only if they are roped together in the same climbing party, moving towards the same summit where they eventually meet. If that is not so why should it be that, in this century of modern comfort, we could find so much joy in sharing our last morsels of food in the desert? . . . For all of us who have known the great joy of coping with forced landings in the Sahara all other pleasure seemed trifling.

Antoine de St. Exupéry

Without the horizon of the highest sacrifice, all sacrifice becomes senseless.

Vaclav Havel

Whoever cares for his own safety is lost; but if a man will let himself be lost for my sake, he will find his true self.

Matthew 16:25

36

THE VULNERABLE

Life persists in the vulnerable, the sensitive. They carry on. The invulnerable, the too heavily armoured perish. Fearful, ill-adapted, cumbersome, impersonal. Dinosaurs and men in tanks. They are so heavily armoured that if they get thrown they will never rise to their feet again without assistance.

Anon.

Finally there is a kind of authority rarely understood, but one into which Christians may be expected to have some special insight. We may call it the authority of vulnerability or openness. Everyone in a position of responsibility is open to attack – often from many different quarters. He therefore tends to surround himself with defences. There is the defence of remoteness, of the use of intermediaries, of didactic attitudes, of seeking popularity by a too easy readiness to compromise, of relying on rules and legal sanctions, of suppressing criticism. These and many others are common defence mechanisms and they have all been part of the stock-in-trade of teachers throughout human history. And all are now being called in question.

This means that although the teacher is still 'in authority' in

view of his function as teacher, and may be 'an authority' on certain matters of fact, his stance in relation to the pupil is not 'authoritarian' . . . This different attitude . . . although it may at first sight appear to expose him to ridicule, in fact often removes the main cause of defensiveness and authoritarian attitudes in the teacher – the fear that he will be discovered not to know something, or not to have the answer the pupil expects from him. To become vulnerable may therefore be a source of strength, though that does not necessarily make it easy to take the plunge.
Christian Commitment in Education.

True history is the history of the spirit, the human spirit which may at times seem powerless but ultimately is yet superior and survives, because even if it has not got the might, it still possesses the power, the power that can never cease.
Leo Baeck

Suppose that, in an opinion poll, we were asked to name the most powerful person in the world: most would probably mention the President of the United States because he disposes of the greatest military machine. If someone suggested that Mother Teresa was the most powerful person, that would no doubt be received with some astonishment. If the same question had been asked in Judea at the time of Jesus the answer would have been the Roman Emperor or locally, his representative Pontius Pilate. Anyone who suggested the gentle prophet from Nazareth in Gallilee would have been thought slightly mad. Surely after his crucifixion it was clear where the power lay. Or was it? Being a Christian involves a reversal of worldly values.

Do not be conformed to this world but be transformed by the renewal of your mind.
Romans 12:2

And from reflection on that cross there has dawned upon the mind of man a new vision of God – a vision of a God who Himself enters into the world's pain, and thereby breaks the power of the world's sin. And with this has gone a new perception of the possibilities of pain – an apprehension that there is a kind and quality of pain that is creative, curative, redemptive, and that this is a kind of pain which man is privileged to share with God. Evil is neither explained nor denied; it is defeated. 'Christianity thus gave to souls the faith and strength to grasp life's nettle.'

B.H. Streeter

The magnificent and pitiful family of the highly sensitive is the salt of the earth. It is they and not others who have founded religions and created masterpieces. The world will never know all that it owes to them, nor above all how much they have suffered in order to give it.

Antoine de St. Exupéry

> Thought shall be the harder,
> Heart the keener,
> Mood shall be the more,
> As our might lessens.
>
> *The Lay of the Battle of Maldon*

He said not – 'Thou shalt not be tempested, thou shalt not be travailed, thou shalt not be dis-eased': but he said: 'Thou shalt not be overcome'.

Julian of Norwich

> Anyone who is chosen, for society's need,
> to be a cabinet member,
> to be president of the republic,
> to be archbishop –
> to be a servant –
> is the servant of God's people.
> That must not be forgotten.
> The attitude to be taken in these offices is not
> 'I'm in charge here! What I want must be done.'
> You are only a human being, God's servant.
> You must be at the Lord's beck and call
> to serve the people according to God's will
> and not according to your whim.
>
> *Oscar Romero*

The power of love is different in nature from the power of domination; it is fragile, vulnerable, conquering through its weakness and its capacity for giving and forgiveness. Jesus

always demonstrated this . . . in his life. He renounced power as domination; he preferred to die in weakness rather than use his power to subjugate people to accept his message . . . It is in weakness that the love of God and the God of love are revealed.
Leonardo Boff

Weakness means suffering; and suffering means sharing; and sharing means exposure.
David Grossman

Is there within and beyond the universe any coherence or meaning or pattern or sovereignty? The New Testament doctrine is that in the death and resurrection of Jesus, in the fact of living through dying, of finding life through losing it, of the saving of self through the giving of self, there is this sovereignty. And to believe it with more than a bare intellectual consent is to believe it existentially, and to believe it existentially is to follow the way of finding life through losing it.
Michael Ramsey

Those apparently powerless individuals who have the courage to speak the truth out loud and stand by what they say body and soul, and are prepared to pay dearly for doing so, have – astonishingly enough – greater power – however formally disfranchised they are – than thousands of anonymous electors in other circumstances.
Vaclav Havel

God chose the foolish things of the world to shame the wise; God chose the weak things of the world to shame the strong.
1 Corinthians 1:27

The Christian walks always in this life by trust and not by sight. And he is content to close his *Te Deum*, his most confident affirmation of faith, with the prayer of vulnerability: 'O Lord, in thee have I *trusted*: let me never be confounded.'
John A.T. Robinson

> Mock on, mock on, Voltaire, Rousseau;
> Mock on, mock on, 'tis all in vain!
> You throw the sand against the wind,
> And the wind blows it back again.
> *William Blake*

37

SUFFERING

Contemplate for a moment a single 'act of God': there has been an earthquake, and in a young family of three the father has been killed at once; the mother dies, in noisy anguish, during the next twenty-four hours; the child, pinned down uninjured between his dead parents, dies slowly of thirst during the next five days, while the bodies of his parents putrify to each side of him . . .

Every justification of God's ways to man proposes some covert and glorious end which more than atones for the overt and outrageous means. But it is among our sharpest moral perceptions that not even the most superb end can justify such means as the killing of this child in these circumstances.

Philip Toynbee

So long as there is a single heart in the world undergoing certain kinds of suffering, a single body experiencing the agony of death, that will demand justification; so long as there remains the suffering of a single child; and so long as even only the animals suffer on earth, that, all that, will demand reparation.

Raissa Maritain.

Those who believe that they believe in God, but without passion in the heart, without anguish of mind, without uncertainty, without doubt and even, at times, without despair, believe only in the idea of God, not in God Himself.

Miguel de Unamuno.

In the last chapter of *The Rebel*, Albert Camus . . . describes two crucial basic experiences of man: evil and death. There we read: 'Rebellion indefatigably confronts evil, from which it can only derive a new impetus.' Man should 'rectify in creation everything that can be rectified. And after he has done so, children will still die unjustly even in a perfect society. Even by his greatest effort, man can only propose to diminish, arithmetically, the sufferings of the world. But the injustice and the suffering of the world will remain and, no matter how limited they are, they will not cease to be an outrage. Dmitri Karamazov's cry of "Why?" will continue to resound through history.'

This question why ... drives the question of an ultimate meaning and a definitive fulfilment away from the fields of conflict on this earth and provides material for all the images of hope, the portrayals of longing, the visions of fulfilment. But this hope is saved from being a feeble illusion ... only if hope and consolation are combined with a realistic enlightenment of man in regard to himself. As against the suspicion of illusion on the part of Freud and all critics of religion, I have tried to bring out the unmasking function of religion itself, admittedly of a purified, responsible religion. That is to say, only a person who has been deprived of illusions about himself in belief in God as the latter showed himself in the cross and resurrection of Jesus Christ, only someone like this is admitted into the following of the Nazarene, someone who will not permit the earth to degenerate into hell, but seeks to make it visible here and now as part of the coming kingdom of God.

Hans Küng

This is the most difficult question of all for religious people – not so much the question of meaningful suffering where we can see, or at least hope, that good will come of it, but the question of apparently meaningless suffering, like the death of the child described by Philip Toynbee. We can only admit that such things are beyond our understanding, that 'Dmitri Karamazov's cry of "Why?" will continue to resound through history'.

What then? Do we abandon our faith that life has meaning and revert to the cynicism of the writer of Ecclesiastes: 'Emptiness, Emptiness, says the Speaker, emptiness, all is empty'. (Eccles 1:2)

The mood of the disciples after the death of Jesus could well have been something like this. Yet they came through it to a serene and joyful faith that what appeared to be a meaningless defeat was in fact a triumphant victory. This choice is the most testing that any of us has to face: it is a matter of decision, sometimes made in total darkness.

If there are ranks in suffering, Israel takes precedence of all the nations; if the duration of sorrows and the patience with which they are borne ennoble, the Jews can challenge the aristocracy of every land; if a literature is called rich in the possession of a few classic tragedies – what shall we say to a national tragedy lasting for fifteen hundred years, in which the poets and the actors were also the heroes?

Leopold Zunz

The Rabbis say: If anyone comes nowadays, and desires to become a proselyte, they say to him: 'Why do you want to become a proselyte? Do you not know that the Israelites are harried, hounded, persecuted and harrassed, and that sufferings befall them?' If he says: 'I know it, and I am not worthy,' they receive him without further argument.

Yebamot

The crucified one was to be found with his own people (the Jews) in the ghettoes, not with those who put the Cross on their banners.

Richard Harries

Whenever pain is so borne as to be prevented from breeding bitterness or any other evil fruit, a contribution is made to rescuing God's creation from the devil's grip.

Leonard Hodgson

For seven days and seven nights they sat beside him on the ground, and none of them said a word to him; for they saw that his suffering was very great.

Job 2:13

Wasserman sees sensitivity to suffering and consciousness of it as the highest goal of mankind. Moreover, it is man's protest, and the highest expression of his freedom. The measure of man's humanity, in Wasserman's opinion, is defined by the amount of suffering he succeeds in diminishing or preventing.

David Grossman

> About suffering they were never wrong,
> The Old Masters: how well they understood
> Its human position; how it takes place
> While someone else is eating or opening a window or
> just walking dully along.
>
> W.H. Auden

Many wounds are inflicted and received simply because someone's general dissatisfaction with life must express itself and the one who happens to be near enough to be hurt is simply unlucky.

Neville Ward

> Most wretched men
> Are cradled into poetry by wrong:
> They learn in suffering what they teach in song.
>
> P.B. Shelley

No greater glory could He have granted to His own, no higher privilege can the Christian enjoy, than to suffer 'for Christ' . . . Blessed is he whom God deems worthy to suffer for the Body of Christ. Such suffering is joy indeed.

Dietrich Bonhoeffer

There is a strength learned from suffering that cannot be learned any other way. For suffering tests the depth of our love of life and relationship even when and especially because relationships are so often the cause of our suffering.

Matthew Fox

It would perhaps be appropriate to consider Christ's attitude towards life, to let it influence your spirit. I have often realized what courage to live, what inner harmony he brought to bear upon his fate, and what joy burned in his heart. He truly lived out the condition of the world, endured it all to the very end. I sense what that meant for him in the hour of Gethsemane. If you think of all this, you may shudder at the thought of what it meant there to 'face life with courage'. There it becomes clear what inner vitality means: the attitude that says ever again 'Nonetheless' and, despite everything that may seem senseless in life, takes up the struggle against sadness.

Trying to be a Christian means letting your mood be ruled by this attitude of Christ, even when you have every reason to be discouraged and despairing. If you could only sense the joy of Christ – that depth of cheerfulness and goodwill – then you would be cheerful your whole life long.

Ladislaus Boros

Then one of the elders asked me, 'These in white robes – who are they, and where did they come from?'

I answered, 'Sir, you know.'

And he said, 'These are they who have come out of the great tribulation; they have washed their robes and made them white in the blood of the Lamb. Therefore, they are before the throne of God and serve him day and night in his temple; and he who sits on the throne will spread his tent over them.

Never again will they hunger; never again will they thirst. The sun will not beat upon them, not any scorching heat.

For the Lamb at the centre of the throne will be their shepherd; he will lead them to springs of living water.

And God will wipe away every tear from their eyes.'

Revelation 7:13–17

38

FORTITUDE

'If a citizen lacks fortitude he becomes a slave and causes immeasurable harm not only to himself but to his family, his country and the Church ... Fortitude is an essential part of one's life as a citizen. That is why fortitude is, for a Christian, the most important duty after love.'

Jerzy Popieluszko

The heroism of the martyrs had consisted of just this: 'They really loved this life; yet they weighed it up. They thought of how much they should love the things eternal; if they were capable of so much love for things that pass away ...'

Augustine of Hippo

The lesson of such stories (of Anton Schmidt, a sergeant in the German Army, who helped the Jewish partisans in Poland and was executed) is simple and within everybody's grasp. Politically speaking, it is that under conditions of terror most people will comply but some people will not, just as the lesson of the countries to which the Final Solution was proposed is that 'it could happen' in most places but it did not happen everywhere. Humanly speaking, no more is required, and no more can reasonably be asked, for this planet to remain a place fit for human habitation.

Hannah Arendt

Someone could say that because Christ was crucified he lost. But he has been winning for 2000 years. The fact that I lose today because someone breaks my jaw or hangs me does not mean I have lost.

Lech Walesa

Patočka once wrote that a life not willing to sacrifice itself to what makes it meaningful is not worth living.

Vaclav Havel

The following is an extract from the sermon preached by Thomas à Becket on Christmas Morning 1170, just before his murder on December 29th, as it is imagined by T.S. Eliot in his play Murder in the Cathedral:

'Beloved, we do not think of a martyr simply as a good Christian who has been killed because he is a Christian: for that would be solely to mourn. We do not think of him simply as a good Christian who has been elevated to the company of the Saints: for that would be simply to rejoice: and neither our mourning nor our rejoicing is as the world's is. A Christian martyrdom is no accident. Saints are not made by accident. Still less is a Christian martyrdom the effect of a man's will to become a Saint, as a man by willing and contriving may become a ruler of men. Ambition fortifies the will of man to become ruler over other men: it operates with deception, cajolery, and violence, it is the action of impurity upon impurity. Not so in heaven. A martyr, a saint, is always made by the design of God, for His love of men, to warn them and to lead them, to bring them back to His ways. A martyrdom is never the design of man; for the true martyr is he who has become the instrument of God, who has lost his will in the will of God, not lost it but found it, for he has found freedom in submission to God. The martyr no longer desires anything for himself, not even the glory of martyrdom. So thus as on earth the Church mourns and rejoices at once, in a fashion that the world cannot understand; so in Heaven the Saints are most high, having made themselves most low, seeing themselves not as we see them, but in the light of the Godhead from which they draw their being.

T.S. Eliot

On 29th May, 1982 the Pope and the Archbishop of Canterbury prayed together at the Chapel of the Modern Martyrs in Canterbury Cathedral. The names of those commemorated there are:

Oscar Romero   *Janani Luwum*   *Maria Skobtsova*
Maximilian Kolbe   *Martin Luther King*
              Dietrich Bonhoeffer

The word 'martyr' means 'witness'. In the early church the martyrs were the faithful witnesses who resisted to the death the tyranny of the Roman Empire. Those who resisted and survived torture often became the leaders of the local churches. The focus of Christian thought was total commitment to the Way of Jesus.

There are thousands of Christians throughout the world to-day who are witnesses (or martyrs) in that same sense. They are remaining faithful to the Way of Jesus at the risk of persecution, imprisonment, torture and death.

Almighty God, by your grace your martyrs shine as lights in the darkness of our times; grant that we may be so encouraged by their example and strengthened by their prayers, that we, too, may bear witness boldly to Christ, who is the Light of life: through Jesus Christ, our Lord.
Prayer in the Chapel of the Saints and Martyrs of our own time in Canterbury Cathedral

Discipleship means allegiance to the suffering Christ, and it is therefore not at all surprising that Christians should be called upon to suffer. In fact it is a joy and a privilege, and a token of His grace. The acts of the early Christian martyrs are full of evidence which shows how Christ glorifies His own in the hour of their mortal agony by granting them the unspeakable assurance of His presence. In the hour of the cruellest torture they bear for His sake, they are made partakers in the perfect joy and bliss of fellowship with Him. To bear the cross proves to be the only way of triumphing over suffering. This is true for all who follow Christ, just as it was true for Him.
Dietrich Bonhoeffer

We must say to our white brothers all over the south who try to keep us down: 'We will match your capacity to inflict suffering with our capacity to endure it. We will meet your physical force with soul force. We will not hate you. And yet we cannot in all good conscience obey your evil laws. Do to us what you will. Threaten our children and we will still love you . . . Say that we're too low, that we're too degraded, yet we will still love you . . . Bomb our homes and . . . our churches . . . and we will still love you. We will wear you down with our capacity to suffer. In winning the victory we will not only win our freedom. We will so appeal to your heart and your conscience that we will win you in the process'.

Martin Luther King

Jean-Bertrand Aristide – President of Haiti

He is a small man, 38 years old, myopic and softly spoken. But in the pulpit he was transformed. His sermons theatrical, poetic, were rallying calls to justice.

They would come on Sundays in their hundreds, walking wounded from the misery of daily life, and 'Titid' would make them feel like the centre of the universe. From his pulpit he denounced the rich, the army, the Pope, the Americans, the successive dictatorships that followed the fall of 'Baby Doc' and the hierarchy of his own Catholic Church . . .

One Sunday, in September 1988 at 9 a.m., they came and burned his church as he was saying Mass. They surrounded it and opened fire, then doused it with kerosene. It is a common feature of such occasions in Haiti that nobody knows how many died . . . the ruin is still there and Mass is still celebrated under the open sky.

They used to say that there were three things you needed to become President of Haiti: l'argent, l'armée and les Americains (money, the army and the U.S.). Aristide had none of them . . . 'And then God will descend' Aristide had preached, 'and put down the mighty and send them away. And he will raise up the lowly and put them on high'. (Luke 1:52)

The scale of his victory was such that no one could dispute it.

'How did Aristide become President?' His friend Father Antoine Adrian replies 'He suffered a great deal. So they called him a prophet. He is utterly charismatic. He gave people hope.'

Isabel Hilton

> She never undertook to know
> What death with love should have to doe;
> Nor has she e'er yet understood
> Why to show love, she should shed blood
> Yet though she cannot tell you why,
> She can LOVE, and she can DY.
>
> Richard Crawshaw
(of St. Theresa of Avila)

VI
MATURITY

39

SPONTANEITY

There were, for Jesus, three stages in the life of man: the unconscious life of the child, the conscious life of the man, and the new life of the member of the Kingdom. In the unconscious life of the child there was spontaneity and wholeness; in the conscious life of the man there was inhibition and division: in the new life of the member of the Kingdom there was spontaneity and wholeness once more.

Middleton Murray

The centre of life is neither in thought nor in feeling nor in will, nor even in consciousness, so far as it thinks, feels, or wishes. For moral truth may have been penetrated and possessed in all these ways, and escape us still. Deeper even than consciousness there is our being itself, our very substance, our nature. Only these truths which have entered into this last region, which have become ourselves, become spontaneous and involuntary, instinctive and unconscious, are really our life – that is to say, something more than our property. So long as we are able to distinguish any space whatever between the truth and us we remain outside it. The thought the feeling, the desire, the consciousness of life, are not yet quite life. But peace and repose can nowhere be found except in life and in eternal life, and the eternal life is the Divine life, is God.

Henri Frédéric Amiel

I live, yet not I, but Christ liveth in me.

Galatians 2:20

'Jesus never acted from policy or deliberation. He never set out to be useful. His acts and thoughts burst out in utterly spontaneous love, abandoning His whole soul to the present, because the present is eternal . . .'

T.S. Gregory

All that the follower of Jesus has to do is to make sure that his obedience, following and love are entirely spontaneous and unpremeditated. If you do good, you must not let your left hand know what your right hand is doing, you must be quite unconscious of it. Otherwise you are simply displaying your own virtue, and not that which has its source in Jesus Christ.

Dietrich Bonhoeffer

Is this spontaneous goodness really possible for humankind? Is it to expect perfection here on earth? John Wesley spoke and wrote about 'perfect love', but later had his doubts. St Augustine too concluded that after conversion we were still sinners. What then is Christian freedom – the 'freedom of the children of God'? Is it freedom from the burden *of sin i.e. a sense of sins forgiven? Continually and unconditionally forgiven?*

So I saw in my Dream, that just as Christian came up with the Cross, his burden loosed from off his Shoulders, and fell from off his back, and began to tumble; and so continued to do, till it came to the mouth of the Sepulchre, where it fell in, and I saw it no more.

Then was Christian glad and lightsome, and said with a merry heart, He hath given me rest, by his sorrow; and life, by his death.

Bunyan

Browning certainly believed in this new freedom:

Let us not always say
    'Spite of this flesh to-day
I strove, made head, gained ground upon the whole'

As the bird wings

and sings

let us cry, 'all good things

Are ours, nor soul helps

flesh more now than

flesh helps soul!'

What is realisation of the self? Idealistic philosophers have believed that self-realisation can be achieved by intellectual insight alone. They have insisted on splitting human personality, so that man's nature may be suppressed and guarded by his reason. The result of this split, however, has been that not only the emotional life of man but also his intellectual faculties have been crippled . . . We believe that the realisation of the self is accomplished not only by an act of thinking but also by the realisation of man's total personality, by the active expression of his emotional and intellectual potentialities. These potentialities are present in everybody; they become real only to the extent to which they are expressed. In other words, positive freedom consists in the spontaneous activity of the total, integrated personality . . .

Small children offer an instance of spontaneity. They have an ability to feel and think that which is really *theirs*; this spontaneity shows in what they say and think, in the feelings that are expressed in their faces. If one asks what makes for the attraction small children have for most people I believe that, apart from sentimental and conventional reasons, the answer may be that it is this very quality of spontaneity . . .

If the individual realises his self by spontaneous activity and thus relates himself to the world, he ceases to be an isolated atom; he and the world become part of one structuralised whole; he has his rightful place, and thereby his doubt concerning himself and the meaning of life disappears. This doubt sprang from his separateness and from the thwarting of life; when he can live, neither compulsively nor automatically but spontaneously, the doubt disappears. He is aware of himself as an active and creative individual and recognises that there is only one meaning of life: the act of living itself . . .

Erich Fromm

THE VICAR QUESTIONS 6 YEAR OLD ANNA

Do you believe in God?
Yes

Do you know what God is?
Yes.

What is God then?
He's . . . God.

Do you go to Church?
No.

Why not?
Because I know it all.

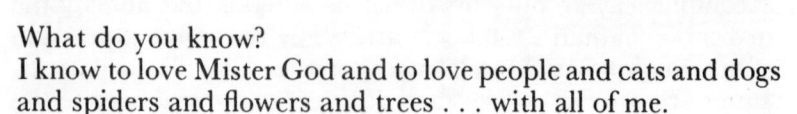

What do you know?
I know to love Mister God and to love people and cats and dogs and spiders and flowers and trees . . . with all of me.

Fynn

At this time the disciples came to Jesus and said, 'Who is the greatest in the kingdom of heaven?' So he called a little child to him and set the child in front of them. Then he said, 'I tell you solemnly, unless you change and become like little children you will never enter the kingdom of heaven.

Matthew 18.1–3

It is not so much a question of finding a *meaning* for life, which is cerebral, as having an *experience of living* here and now.

Joseph Campbell

Woman represents the value-claims of present sensuous immediacy ... Masculine reason consciously distances itself from and seeks to control everything that is immediate, volatile, female, emotional and natural.

Don Cupitt

Don Cuppit suggests that this sexist division, which he traces back to the Greek distinction between reason and the passions and belongs to the past, must be overcome. There will be more women scientists and politicians and more domesticated men, more women capable of planning for the future, more men capable of enjoying the here and now.

Technology and administration in various ways require us to split and devalue Being by thinking of things instrumentally and in terms of control. We divide form and matter, theory and experience, reason and the passions, fact and value, proximate and remote, means and ends and so on. Our religion will cultivate a wisdom that undoes these distinctions in a spiritual movement of reconciliation. Life is fully returned to itself. Value flows back in. Being in all its plenitude is experienced in the fleeting instant.

Our religion, then, will be a training in contemplative wisdom that teaches us how to look at the world in a truly religious way. It will be a post-historical vision, in that it does not look to any future vindication but rather itself vindicates everything right now. Nor are we talking about anything that is in the least esoteric. On the contrary it is something that every artist, every mystical tradition, and every great faith already knows.

We should be training our senses, praying with our eyes open and learning to see the world whole. We don't need introspective retreats; we need art-retreats and nature-retreats.

Don Cuppit

40

THE GREATNESS OF SMALL ACTIONS

He who would do good to another must do it in minute particulars.

William Blake

In order to do good to others he would have needed besides the principles that filled his mind, an unprincipled heart – the kind of heart that knows of no general cases but only particular ones, and has the greatness of small actions.

Boris Pasternak

A civilization may be wrecked without any spectacular crimes or criminals but by constant petty breaches of faith and minor complicities on the part of men generally considered very nice people. If we were to imagine a great war taking place, say in 1960, we who often measure guilt by its consequences might well be wrong in imagining that a tragedy so stupendous could only be the work of some special monster of wickedness. If all men had only what we consider a reasonable degree of cupidity, politics would still be driven into dialectical jams – into predicaments and dilemmas which the intellect has never mastered. If there were no more wilfulness throughout the whole of human nature than exists in this room at the present moment, it would be sufficient to tie events into knots and produce those deadlocks which all of us know in our little world, while on the scale of the nation-state it would be enough . . . to bring about the greatest war in history.

Herbert Butterfield

My religion consists of a humble admiration for the Superior Spirit who reveals Himself in the slight details we are able to perceive with our frail and feeble minds.
Albert Einstein

As for me, my bed is made: I am against bigness and greatness in all their forms, and with the invisible molecular forces that work from individual to individual, stealing in through the crannies of the world like so many soft rootlets, or like the capillary oozing of water, and yet rending the hardest monument of man's pride if you give them time. I am against all big organizations as such, national ones first and foremost; against all big successes and big results; and in favour of the eternal forces of truth which always work in the individual and immediately unsuccessful way, under-dogs always, till history comes after they are long dead and puts them on top.
William James

Wisdom (i.e. holiness) consists in doing the next thing you have to do, doing it with your whole heart, and finding delight in doing it.
Meister Eckhart

An easy task becomes difficult when you do it with reluctance.
Terence

A difficult task may become easy when you do it with love.

Jesus did not act from a well-defined concept of ... final salvation. Rather, he saw a distant vision of final, perfect and universal salvation – the kingdom of God – *in and through* his own *fragmentary actions*, which were historical and thus limited or finite, 'going around doing good' through healing, liberating from demonic powers, and reconciliation. Understood in the way, Jesus did not live by a utopian, distant vision or by a consummation of all things in God which had already been brought about 'ideally', but he recognized in his specific action of doing good a practical anticipation of salvation to come. This confirms the *permanent validity* of any practice of doing good which is incomplete because it is historically limited.
Edward Schillebeeckx

An essential part of the 'dissident' attitude is that it comes out of the reality of the human 'here and now'. It places more importance on often repeated and consistent concrete action – even though it may be inadequate and though it may ease only insignificantly the suffering of a single insignificant citizen – than it does in some abstract 'fundamental solution' in an uncertain future.

Vaclav Havel

A friend told me she had no experience of the Holy Spirit – no sense of religious ecstasy, no speaking with tongues, no gift of oratory. When I suggested that each time she picked up an elderly or disabled person in her car to take them to do their shopping, to go to church or hospital (as she often did) that could be the work of the Holy Spirit in her, she was astonished that anything so mundane could be so regarded, but was now grateful that the Spirit had not, as she had thought, altogether neglected her.

We could all make a list of small actions which have remained in our memory and therefore influenced our lives. They often make a deeper impression than dramatic gestures.

On visiting a convent I saw a nun polishing a door-handle: she did not look up as we passed so engrossed was she in making that handle shine for the glory of God.

Once, when my wife was seriously ill, there was a ring at the door. A neighbour who looked after fourteen deprived children was there offering me a large baked custard she had made because she thought I might be having some difficulty in preparing my meals.

When my wife died a friend I met in the street put her arm round me and, without saying a word, walked on.

My doctor, whom I had not seen for some months, took the trouble to call at my rather remote house and, as I was out, left a note saying, 'Can I be of any help?'

The marvels of God's activity which delight us when we read about them only serve to make us bored with the small happenings around us. Yet it is these trivialities, as we consider them, which would do marvels for us if only we did not despise them. We are so stupid!

J.P. de Caussade

The Gospel parable of the talents was not told for the benefit of those who have five talents or those who have two, but for those who have only one and see no potential in it. In fact our religious tradition is rich in reminders of the significance of the insignificant: the still small voice, the one coin lost, the grain of mustard seed, the single sparrow that falls to the ground.

Edward Robinson

>I come in the little things
>Saith the Lord:
>My starry wings
>I do forsake,
>Love's highway of humility to take:
>Meekly I fit My stature to your need.
>In begger's part
>About your gates I shall not cease to plead –
>As man, to speak with man –
>Till by such art
>I shall achieve my immemorial plan,
>Pass the low lintel of the human heart.
>
>*Evelyn Underhill*

Peace is a universal responsibility; it comes about through a thousand little acts in daily life!

Pope John Paul II

41

LEARNING/MATURITY

The patterns of community life have a more potent educational influence than any formal schooling.
The Churches survey their task.

I am going to risk your smiles by defining an adult as a person who has at last grown able to rely upon himself as teachable. The physical grown-ups who are not adult in this sense are still fundamentalists, feeling out to life and the unknown reluctantly and spasmodically. They are never clear thinkers, although they may hold first class degrees, never surrendered pupils to life, the school of values and relationships and daily dying into something ever simpler and fuller.
George Lyward

The real secret of living in a Home with children is to know how to be creative in taking away and in being 'unfair' and haphazard, so that the gift shall never deny the children increasing awareness of the giver.
George Lyward

This learning to live means, not just a patching up or a getting rid of some 'objectionable traits', but a gradual and infinitely thorough re-creation. As they abandon their pretences and go back to a new beginning, the boys are gently 'weaned', 'loosened', 'healed', given back their lives which in some way have been 'usurped'. It is generally the parents who have taken away the boy's own life and forced him into a world of fantasy. Perhaps they do this by continued absence abroad and consequent 'abandonment'; by failing to develop a spontaneous relationship with their son; by a constant harping on moral standards that have no meaning for the child; or by their insistence that he should 'get on' and be a success.

George Lyward

George Lyward, who made such perceptive and challenging comments about relationships with disturbed adolescents, spent most of his life as 'chief' of a community for the maladjusted. His comment about being 'unfair' has often been misunderstood. Fairness is often interpreted as treating all alike. But individuals are different; their needs are different, and to treat them all alike is to ignore those differences. In this sense it is essential to be unfair – to relate to each individual as he or she is at that moment, not as a numerical unit in a group of identical clones.

The insights Lyward gained through his courageously independent and unconventional methods have influenced many workers in that field and fundamentally changed the understanding of adolescents in their relationships both with adults (especially parents) and their peers. He saw those relationships and lived them always 'in depth' – at the level of the unconscious rather than the conscious mind – realising that damage done at the unconscious level (e.g. in infancy) can only be healed at that same level. Similar insights concerning the unconscious are found in the quotations from William Temple, Simone Weil, and Gabriel Moran. Lyward's originality was to apply those insights to the healing of the maladjusted. They have important implications for the upbringing of children, for education in general and for the meaning of maturity.

We have to expose ourselves to the animal impulses of the unconscious without identifying ourselves with them and without running away.

C.G. Jung

Especially in early childhood, when there is no critical capacity, and the soul is therefore in the highest degree sensitive to influences, the formative power of the family is incalculable. Here the two requisites are simply goodness of character and love. A child is very imitative. But quite unconsciously it imitates the spirit rather than the outward act. A child surrounded by love will tend to become loving; and a child surrounded by selfishness will tend to become selfish.

The selfish parent may be either 'kind' or 'cruel' or both (for both are rather pleasing things to be); but whichever form the selfishness takes, it is the selfishness that will be imparted. The loving parents may be gentle or stern, or more probably both, for both are at different times in place, but through either the gentleness or the sternness the love will tell, and it is the love that will be imparted. No rules for conduct can be given; kindness will not 'spoil' nor sternness save; but love will save and selfishness will spoil.

William Temple

A child hungry for love is most quick to detect and reject condescension, bribery or manipulation when it masquerades as love, and requires most full assurance of the authenticity of that which is offered to him. Though he has never tasted authentic love, he knows already the taste of what he needs.

W.H. Vanstone

Gradually over the past twenty years (as an Inspector of Schools) I had come to see that my own views were totally opposed to our educational system, and I had often found myself in the enemy's camp. As our society was becoming increasingly competitive, and success was measured materially ... the great unmeasurable qualities of feeling, of personal creativity, of discrimination, of sensitive awareness of others, and of dedicated service seemed more and more to be regarded as lesser by-products, commendable but unimportant. The few children who were academically bright – which, more than anything meant that they had retentive memories and could regurgitate the factual knowledge poured into them – were fostered at the expense of the majority: and schools still tended to be valued according to what are called 'results,' though everyone knows that the true results of education only show with maturity. 'The system' was designed to create an elite – and, moreover, a not truly educated, cultivated, vital elite.

So I was determined to be even more outspoken in my beliefs, leaving no school or college in any doubt as to where I stood and what I considered should be our priorities. I would strive only that ordinary children and ordinary teachers should realise their gifts and powers. For the less favourably endowed make up the great majority of our people, and only by broadening their attitudes and raising their standards can ours become a more enlightened country.

R. Tanner

To have spiritual authority is to have been there oneself, and to have come back. The point is not, most emphatically, that we can employ either the priest or the artist to do something on our behalf, to save ourselves the trouble. Quite the contrary, what they can do, all they can do, is show, first, that it is possible, and then, that the journey, that transcendence, is required of us all.

Edward Robinson

The key to a Christian conception of learning is that prayer is attention. It is the turning towards God of all the attention of which the soul is capable. The quality of attention counts for much in the quality of prayer. Warmth of heart cannot take its place. It is the element of desire in learning which can make it a preparation for the spiritual life. For desire, directed towards God, is the only force capable of uplifting the soul.

Attention consists in suspending one's thought and leaving it available, empty and penetrable by the object of our attention; in maintaining in proximity to our thought, but at a lower level and without direct contact with it, the different parcels of acquired knowledge that we are bound to make use of. In relation to all previously formulated particular thoughts, our thought must be like a man on a mountain who, while looking straight before him, notices simultaneously beneath him, without looking at them directly, many forests and plains. And above all our thought must be empty, expectant, without seeking anything specific, but ready to receive in its naked truth the object which is about to enter into it.

Simone Weil

In natural knowledge knowing and being can be separate: a lepidopterist does not need to be a butterfly. But with connatural knowledge to know and to be cannot be separate; they are two aspects of the one act.

Donald Nicholl

Everything in the child's early experience that contributes to his development as a human being is also a foundation for his adult Christian life. There can no longer be any doubt about the importance of the 'education of the unconscious' and of creating the milieu in which the emotional responsiveness of the child can flower. This should always have been demanded by the nature of Christian revelation, but when revelation tended to be identified with concepts, propositions, and doctrines, it was supposed that early religious education was not very important. Our study of the theology of revelation joins forces with the findings of modern psychology in emphasizing the crucial significance of the budding religious life of the small child.

There is no way to explain to a small child what it means to be a Christian; it can only be demonstrated.

Gabriel Moran

And He put his arms round them, laid his hands upon them, and blessed them.

Mark 10:16

42

FREEDOM

Then Moses said to the people, 'Remember this day, the day on which you have come out of Egypt, the land of slavery, because the Lord by the strength of his hand has brought you out.
Exodus 13.3

Christ set us free, to be free men. Stand firm then and refuse to be tied to the yoke of slavery again.
Galatians 5:1

Live as free men; not however as though your freedom were there to provide a screen for wrongdoing, but as slaves in God's service.
1 Peter 2:16

This is a well known Christian paradox which Luther expressed in two guiding principles:
   'A Christian is a free master over all things and subject to no one', *but also*
   'A Christian is a servant at the disposal of all things and subject to everyone'.

   Hans Küng has commented on the first principle:

'This holds for the inward, new, spiritual man: for the man of faith. For man becomes really free, not by any external realities, not by having or doing something externally, not by being concerned with holy things, wearing priestly vestments, performing pious works, observing ecclesiastical customs. No, man becomes free by the word of God itself, by the gospel, on whose promises man can rely. Not any kind of human religious law, human precept, human work, but (and this has scarcely been proclaimed) only trusting faith makes man a Christian, makes him truly free.' . . .

On the second principle he comments:

'For Luther, as at an earlier stage for Paul, man as a person is radically changed by faith. Insofar as it is the expression of God's will, he fulfills the law out of love and consequently goes far beyond what is required. For the believer, God's will is not a coercive, guilt-imposing accusatory law, but a challenging promise, liberating grace: out of faith proceeds love of God and a free, voluntary, joyous life of service to one's neighbor. For the Christian is not expected to do pious works for his own soul's salvation – as devout people, especially in monasteries and convents, often attempt to do – but with faith in Christ and out of love for his neighbor. Thus for Luther, as for Paul at an earlier stage, freedom also involves commitment.'

Both animals and the natural man live in the herd for mutual protection. The cohesion of the herd is based on fear. When, however, we find what Hans Küng calls 'trusting faith' we are freed from fear; we become individual persons, free to act independently of the herd and free, as never before, to commit ourselves to a community no longer based on fear, a community of people who freely commit themselves to each other in love.

Eric Fromm's distinction between the negative and positive aspects of freedom – 'freedom from' and 'freedom to' – makes a similar, though not identical, point in terms of political freedom and its relation to faith in life and in truth – 'freedom as the active and spontaneous realization of the individual self'. But when the individual self has been realized in freedom from external, authoritarian powers, we are 'isolated, alone and afraid' unless we can freely make a commitment to a new community of free persons.

It took over four hundred years to break down the medieval world and to free people from the most apparent restraints. But while in many respects the individual has grown, has developed mentally and emotionally, and participates in cultural achievements in a degree unheard of before, the lag between 'freedom from' and 'freedom to' has grown too. The result of this dis-proportion between freedom *from* any tie and the last of possibilities for the positive realization of freedom and individuality has led, in Europe, to a panicky flight from freedom into new ties or at least into complete indifference.

The structure of modern society affects man in two ways simultaneously: he becomes more independent, self-reliant, and critical, and he becomes more isolated, alone, and afraid.

The negative side of freedom, the burden which it puts upon man, is difficult to realize, especially for those whose heart is with the cause of freedom. . . .

We are fascinated by the growth of freedom from powers outside ourselves and are blinded to the fact of inner restraints, compulsions, and fears, which tend to undermine the meaning of the victories freedom has won against its traditional enemies . . . We not only have to preserve and increase the traditional freedom, but . . . we have to gain a new kind of freedom, one which enables us to realize our own individual self, to have faith in this self and in life.

Man does not suffer so much from poverty to-day as he suffers from the fact that he has become a cog in a large machine, an automaton, that his life has become empty and lost its meaning. The victory over all kinds of authoritarian systems will be possible only if democracy does not retreat but takes the offensive and proceeds to realize what has been its aim in the minds of those who fought for freedom throughout the last centuries. It will triumph over the forces of nihilism only if it can imbue people with a faith that is the strongest the human mind is capable of, the faith in life and in truth, and in freedom as the active and spontaneous realization of the individual self.

Erich Fromm

The reality is that God genuinely does not know the outcome of the creative process. He waits upon the response of his creation. . . . Vanstone recognizes the real freedom of the creative universe where total freedom is the necessary consequence of God's love.

Marcus Braybrooke on W.H. Vanstone

There is only one cure for the evils which newly acquired freedom produces; and that is freedom.

Lord Macaulay

The Grand Inquisitor speaks to Jesus of the temptations:

Remember the first question; its meaning, in other words, was this: Thou wouldst go into the world, and art going with empty hands, with some promise of freedom which men in their simplicity and their natural unruliness cannot even understand, which they fear and dread – for nothing has ever been more insupportable for a man and a human society than freedom. But seest Thou these stones in this parched and barren wilderness? Turn them into bread and mankind will run after Thee like a flock of sheep, grateful and obedient, though for ever trembling, lest Thou withdraw Thy hand and deny them Thy bread. But Thou wouldst not deprive man of freedom and didst reject the offer, thinking, what is that freedom worth, if obedience is bought with bread? Thou didst reply that man lives not by bread alone.

No science will give them bread so long as they remain free. In the end they will lay their freedom at our feet, and say to us, 'Make us your slaves, but feed us.' They will understand themselves, at last, that freedom and bread enough for all are inconceivable together, for never, never will they be able to share between them!

So long as man remains free he strives for nothing so incessantly and so painfully as to find some one to worship. But man seeks to worship what is established beyond dispute, so that all men would agree at once to worship it. . . . This craving for *community* of worship is the chief misery of every man individually and of all humanity from the beginning of time. For the sake of common worship they've slain each other with the sword. They have set up gods and challenged one another, 'Put away your gods and come and worship ours, or we will kill you and your gods!' . . . Thou didst know, Thou couldst not but have known, this fundamental secret of human nature, but Thou didst reject the one infallible banner which was offered Thee to make all men bow down to Thee alone – the banner of earthly bread; and Thou hast rejected it for the sake of freedom and the bread of Heaven.

Didst Thou forget that man prefers peace, and even death, to freedom of choice in the knowledge of good and evil? Nothing is more seductive for man than his freedom of conscience, but nothing is a greater cause of suffering.

Instead of taking possession of man's freedom, Thou didst increase it, and burdened the spiritual kingdom of mankind with its sufferings for ever. Thou didst desire man's free love, that he should follow Thee freely, enticed and taken captive by Thee. In place of the rigid ancient law, man must hereafter with free heart decide for himself what is good and what is evil, having only Thy image before him as his guide. But didst Thou not know he would at last reject even Thy image and Thy truth, if he is weighed down with the fearful burden of free choice?
Fyodor Dostoyevsky

Men who are not free always idealize their bondage.
Boris Pasternak

It is through the tragedy of freedom that Christian renaissance on a world scale will take place. The Christianity of the future will be a Christianity of the freedom of the spirit which has successfully passed through the trials of freedom by overcoming the temptation to refuse them.
Nicholas Berdyaev

Are these dreams of freedom pure illusion? The Grand Inquisitor tells Jesus that they are, that the promise of freedom that Jesus made is an impossible dream: 'Freedom and bread enough for all are inconceivable together, for never, never, will they be able to share between them!' Does it look to-day as though the Grand Inquisitor was right? Is the gap between rich and poor nations, greater than ever? What, if any, are the signs of hope, of a greater readiness to share?

With man this is impossible, but not with God; all things are possible with God.
Mark 10:27

> Make me a captive, Lord,
> And then I shall be free.
George Matheson

> Man is condemned to be free.
Jean Paul Sartre

In their terror they clamoured to the Lord for help and said to Moses, 'Were there no graves in Egypt, that you should have brought us here to die in the wilderness? See what you have done to us by bringing us out of Egypt! Is not this just what we meant when we said in Egypt, "Leave us alone; let us be slaves to the Egyptians"? . . . 'Have no fear,' Moses answered: 'stand firm and see the deliverance that the Lord will bring you this day.'

Exodus 14. 10–13

I have a dream. It is a dream that is deeply rooted in the American dream. I have a dream that one day this nation will rise up, live out the true meaning of its creed: 'We hold these truths to be self-evident, that all men are created equal.'

When we allow freedom to ring from every town and every hamlet, from every state and every city, we will be able to speed up that day when all of God's children, black men and white men, Jews and Gentiles, Protestants and Catholics, will be able to join hands and sing in the words of the old negro spiritual, 'Free at last, free at last, great God Almighty, we are free at last.'

Martin Luther King

In 1688, Britain set itself free, and the energy of that bloodless revolution created the first industrial revolution. In 1776, the United States declared its independence and that liberated the huge energies of America. In 1991, the Russians have freed themselves from communism. There is no limit to the creative potential of these revolutions of human freedom, and no limit to what Russia can achieve in the 21st century.

William Rees-Mogg

Prayer Before Birth

I am not yet born; O fill me
With strength against those who would freeze my
humanity, would dragoon me into a lethal automaton
would make me a cog in a machine, a thing with
one face, a thing, and against all those
who would dissipate my entirety, would
blow me like thistledown hither and
thither or hither and thither

>   like water held in the
>   hands would spill me.
> let them not make me a stone and let them not spill me
>   Otherwise kill me.
>
>   *Louis Macneice*

43

POLITICAL HOLINESS

A controversial title? The main Christian tradition of holiness has been one of personal piety, of inward holiness. John Wesley spoke of his mission to spread 'scriptural holiness' throughout the land: this certainly included social concern such as the visiting of prisoners and charitable care for the poor, but not 'political holiness' as it is understood to-day.

There are martyrs because of their public profession of a faith that de-absolutises and de-divinises the powers of this world, which claim to be the final arbiters. History is full of such martyrs, from the time the Roman emperors were declared divine to those who speak out against modern fascist tyrannies.

There are likewise martyrs on account of their Christian practice derived from following Christ. . . . Not a few Christians (cardinals, bishops, priests, religious and lay people), because of the Gospel, make a preferential option for the poor, for their liberation, for the defence of their rights. In the name of this option they stand up and denounce the exercise of domination and all forms of social dehumanisation. They may be persecuted, arrested, tortured and killed. They, too, are martyrs in the strict sense of the word.

Christians are not normally hated because they call themselves. Christians They are persecuted and hated because they commit themselves to the process of liberation and confess that this commitment comes from their experience of the Gospel and of prayer. It is this connection that is rejected and that provokes the sacrifice of their lives through martyrdom.

Leonardo Boff

Throughout the history of the Church, it has been assumed that the proper environment for holiness is personal ascesis, contemplation, the exercise of charity in the form of alms-giving, etc. Now, because they have become aware of the misery and oppression of the majority of the human race and of the processes of liberation which have been set in motion in the Third World . . . many Christians feel that the area of political action is the right place to seek holiness. This of course does not exclude other ways of seeking holiness, but politics is one possible way and because of the signs of the times it has become an historical necessity.

The political love which seeks to transform the situation of these poor people must have its specific mechanisms, distinct from those belonging to other forms of love; it must seek structural efficacy. It must denounce oppression and unmask its structural causes, plead for basic human, social and political rights, help to bring about 'bold and urgent' structural changes, as Paul VI said.

Jon Sobrino

A better system will not automatically ensure a better life. In fact the opposite is true: only by creating a better life can a better system be developed.

Vaclav Havel

The Kingdom is where earthly, ego-dominated values are turned upside down, so that the dispossessed possess; the have-nots have; the powerful achieve their ambitions; the outcasts are invited in. As Daniel Berrigan puts it:

> Heaven of such imperfection
> Wary, ravaged, wild?
> Yes; compel them in.

The Kingdom is thus the triumph of the last over the first, of the humble over the proud, the ordinary over the exotic. Political spirituality is in part opening the inner self to the presence, the actual and spiritual reality, of these people, the inheritors of the Kingdom. It is being alive to them, welcoming them in, standing alongside them.

Charles Elliot

We begin to find that with individuals, as with nations, the only safe revolution is one arising out of the wants which their *own progress* has generated.

George Eliot

> Only the free have disposition to be truthful,
> Only the truthful have the interest to be just
> Only the just possess the will-power to be free.

W.H. Auden

It must be considered that there is nothing more difficult to carry out, nor more dangerous to handle, than to initiate a new order of things. For the reformer has enemies in all those who profit by the old order, and only lukewarm defenders in all those who would profit by the new order, this lukewarmness arising partly from the incredulity of mankind, who do not truly believe in anything new until they have had actual experience of it.

Nicolo Machiavelli

... for the believer who seeks to follow God, the only orientation for action can be to further the good and to oppose evil, injustice and suffering in all its forms. This conception of God, which is not given to us as the result of a universal concept of God as found in the history of religions, but appears from and in Jesus of Nazareth, communicates to the Christian a quite definite orientation for action ... he has the obligation, in faith, to further what is good and true for a realization of humanity; to fight energetically against everything which vitiates man's physical life, burdens his psychological life, humiliates him as a person, enslaves him through social structures, drives him into an irresponsible adventure through irrationality, makes the free exercise of his religious feeling impossible; and finally, to oppose everything which infringes human rights and reifies men as a result of their working conditions and the bureaucracy which shapes them.

Edward Schillebeeckx

The stifling pall of hollow words that has smothered us for so long has cultivated in us such a deep mistrust of the world of deceptive words that we are now better equipped than ever before to see the human world as it really is: a complex community of thousands of millions of unique, individual human beings, in whom hundreds of beautiful characteristics are matched by hundreds of faults and negative tendencies. They must never be lumped together into homogeneous masses beneath a welter of hollow clichés and sterile words and then *en bloc* – as 'classes', 'nations' or 'political forces' – extolled or denounced, loved or hated, maligned or glorified.

Vaclav Havel

Christian belief in what is humanly impossible, namely a radically new improvement of the world, automatically drives Christians to quite specific political action. For conversion of the heart, on which Christian faith lays so much emphasis, is conditioned by the social structures in which human freedom is contained, and in turn the evil intentions of the human heart influence these structures. There is a dialectical relationship between conversion of the heart and the conversion of social structures, although even with the best possible structures the human heart can still cause disruption and injustice, and although even in unjust structures man personally can rise to the heights of human dignity.

Edward Schillebeeckx

The Christian position may be summed up as follows: in personal matters, powerlessness: in public matters, power for the weak.

Richard Harries

Can we hope that the Church, which has so often supported the rich and powerful, may in our time be finding a new alignment with the poor, the persecuted, the powerless? Not only have many Christians ('cardinals, bishops, priests, religious and lay people') made 'a preferential option for the poor', but, as I write, news comes that the Pope has agreed that Mother Teresa should open a hostel for 'the poorest of the poor' inside the Vatican. The symbolic implications of such news are far reaching indeed. Could it be that the institutional Church itself is, at long last, returning to its Source in the Gospel?

On Sunday the Pope will attend a ceremony to found a hostel for 74 people – the first created within Vatican walls – built on the initiative of Mother Teresa. 'It is intended for the poorest of the poor,' said Mother Teresa. The hostel . . . will consist of dormitories, bathrooms and a refectory where the needy may receive at least one substantial meal everyday . . . It will give particular attention to the homeless, abandoned and distressed who are also handicapped. Those seeking refuge may simply request entrance at the gates of that section of the Vatican.

Newspaper report

Patocka used to say that the most interesting thing about responsibility is that we carry it with us everywhere. That means that responsibility is ours, that we must accept it and grasp it here, now, in this place in time and space where the Lord has set us down, and that we cannot lie our way out of it by moving somewhere else, whether it be to an Indian ashram or to a parallel polis. If Western young people so often discover that retreat to an Indian monastery fails them as an individual or group solution, then this is obviously because, and only because it lacks that element of universality, since not everyone can retire to an ashram. Christianity is an example of an opposite way out: it is a point of departure for me here and now – but only because anyone, anywhere, at any time, may avail themselves of it.

Vaclav Havel

This is what I have felt all my life, that the individual must not wait for Government, and he must not wait for groups and powerful people to do something. He must take care of what is on his doorstep; that is the material that he has in life and he must work with that.

Laurens van der Post

There is neither Jew nor Greek, slave nor free, male nor female, for you are all one in Christ Jesus.

Galations 3:28

'Our citizenship is in Heaven': yes, but that is the model and type for your citizenship upon earth.

T.S. Eliot

44

THE PRESENT MOMENT

'I cannot ope mine eyes
But thou art ready there to catch
My morning soul and sacrifice. . . .'
George Herbert

We can generally know now what he wants us to do *now*. We cannot always know now what he will want us to do in the future. If we are thinking out a problem and light does not come, it is right to regard that as present guidance. Having done all the thinking we fruitfully can about the matter, we have clearly to endure the obscurity of the situation, and we had better leave the perplexing issue and give ourselves to the immediate duty or pleasure that is in front of us. There is always something God wants us to do *now*. It must always be one thing. It must always be something that we can do.
J. Neville Ward

In the state of abandonment the only rule is the duty of the present moment.
J. P. de Caussade

Practising Buddhism is to be alive in each moment. When we practise (meditation) sitting or walking, we have the means to do it perfectly. During the rest of the day, we also practice. It is more difficult, but it is possible. The sitting and the walking must be extended to the non-walking, non-sitting moments of our day. That is the basic principle of meditation.
Thich Nhat Hanh

The only thing that matters is *now*. We have to be exactly in God's will – united actively and passively with what he wants us to be and to do – so that at every moment we are quite simply in touch with God because we are wishing to do what he wants of us and to be as we find he wishes us to be. There is no other perfection than this. To-morrow and yesterday are of quite secondary importance.

Dom John Chapman

The only strength for me is to be found in the sense of a personal presence everywhere, it scarcely matters whether it be called human or divine; a presence which only makes itself felt at first in this and that particular feature. . . . Into this presence we come, *not* by leaving behind what are usually called earthly things, or by loving them less, but by living more intensely in them, and loving more what is really lovable in them; for it is literally true that this world is everything to us, if only we choose to make it so, – if only we 'live in the present' because it is eternity . . .

Anon

Christ waits for us here, at this very time, at this very place, and nowhere else.

Dag Hammarskjold

The power of meditating is that we seek to be fully in the present moment, not thinking about the past, not regretting the past, weeping over it, analysing it. Not planning for the future. God is. God is love. God is now.

In meditation we are simply as wholly and fully open to the love of this present moment as possible.

John Main

Far too many people live too much in their heads – they are mostly conscious of the thinking and fantasizing that is going on in their head and far too little conscious of the activity of their senses. As a result they rarely live in the present. They are almost always in the past or in the future. . . .

To succeed in prayer it is essential to develop the ability to make contact with the present and to stay there. And there is no better method I know of for staying in the present than getting out of your head and returning to your senses.

Anthony de Mello

Where we actually are is where we belong.
Nowness flowers from a situation impossible to live in,

a miraculous bloom out of dry soil.

Thomas Merton

It is only in the present that we can realise the presence.
 On the Sunday after the crucifixion of Jesus two of the disciples were leaving Jerusalem and walking to Emmaus, a distance of about seven miles. (Luke 24. 13–32.) It was natural that they should be preoccupied with the events of the past few days in Jerusalem, events which had shaken the very foundations of their lives. In fact they were so preoccupied with those events that when someone else joined them on the road, they hardly paid any attention to him. Their faces were full of gloom.

There were several reasons for their gloom:

1. They had lost their leader – *the one who had given a sense of direction and purpose to their lives, who had inspired them by his words and actions, by his very presence, by the impact of his warm and vigorous personality.*

   Without him they were lost, lacking motivation from within themselves. While he was with them they thought they knew what he meant by his words. His powerful actions; his faith and confidence in God his Father seemed to rub off on to them. But without him the teaching lacked substance, the words evaporated into thin air, and their confidence seemed no more real or lasting than a dream after waking.

2. *But there was another reason for their gloom* – a sense of guilt. *They were at least partly responsible for what had happened. When things had become really dangerous they had panicked and disappeared from the scene as quietly and quickly as possible. Of course they had not anticipated anything quite as awful as what had actually happened. The soldiers might simply have arrested Jesus for questioning and then let him go. After all, he had committed no crime. How were they to know what was going to happen?*

   Yet, in spite of all the excuses they might make for themselves, the sense of guilt would not go away. It kept on nagging at them and deepened their gloom. It made them so preoccupied with themselves that they were scarcely aware of the one who had joined them. When he drew attention to himself by asking them questions, they could only talk about their own disappointment and depression, without a thought as to who he might be, or what he might require of them.

   One thing, then, which kept them from seeing who it was, was preoccupation with the past and with their own sense of guilt.

3. *They were also concerned* about the future They had lost hope.

   '*We had been hoping that he was the man to liberate Israel.*'

   So what now? The future was dark; there was no sign, no hope now, of any end to the occupation of their land by the Roman forces. Nor of that deeper spiritual liberation of Israel by the Messiah, and the coming of his Kingdom of righteousness and peace – a Kingdom of which they had glimpses, even some actual experience, when Jesus was with them. But what now? Back to square one.

So their concern with the past and their forebodings about the future prevented them from living in the present 'from seeing who it was' who was with them on the road at that very moment.

Is this not often true of us? That our preoccupation with our sense of guilt about the past (whether it be openly acknowledged or hidden even from ourselves, because we dare not face the truth about ourselves), and also our fears about the future often prevent us from living in the present *and so from realising the* presence.

For it is only in the present that we can realise the presence.

45

WESTERN CIVILISATION

He thought of civilised and morally tolerable human life as a dangerous walk on a thin crust of barely cooled lava which at any moment might break and let the unwary sink into fiery depths.

Bertrand Russell on Conrad

In the West there is a drying up of religious consciousness and the sapping of strength from within is even more dangerous than the pressure from without experienced in totalitarian countries. The West has abandoned itself to the pursuit of happiness and religious concepts are being replaced by political systems promising an ever rising standard of living.

Alexander Solzhenitsyn

There can be little question that part of the flight from darkness in the modern period of Western culture has been the flight from mortality and the fear of death, of letting go of this life. Otto Rank sees this fear of death as the most basic characteristic of a patriarchal society. It has much to do with our hatred of animals, of the earth, of life in fact. This fear drives out any Eros or love of life.

Matthew Fox

By nailing a man's whole attention to the floor of his mere consumer interests, it is hoped to render him incapable of appreciating the ever increasing degree of his spiritual, political and moral degradation.

Vaclav Havel

Could it be that this idea that there is no consciousness in the world apart from our own (the gamble of the atheist) is what lays the very foundations of decadence? If events have no reality, why should we take them seriously? If, in everything, we are both judges and plaintiffs, why should we go to court?
Françoise Chandernagor

... there is all the difference in the world between re-establishing a religion in society and re-establishing a society in religion. In the latter case religion is the roots of the tree, in the former it is a mere rookery.
John Taylor

In the expansion and explosion of the West into the world in the last ten centuries, it has acquired, first an expansionist ego, and secondly a deep but subconscious guilt about the aggressive acts in this expansion. The expansionist and extrovert ego has grown into a productive and technological ego. It has created science and technology which is to-day bringing the world together.

The West ... could not have brought out the science and technology which the whole world covets today without serious loss to the inner man. To-day the West finds it painful to look into its own soul and discover the emptiness and the guilt that is written there. But being human it finds itself unable to take the way of brokenness and repentance. Brokenness is antithetical to the activist outlook and so the best it can do is to compensate for its guilt by its goodness.
Paul Verghese

Traditionally, the western approach to law has veered between the ideal and the rather harshly realistic ... The judge would see law as the impartial arbiter, but in hard reality it has been at least as much the tool of the rich and the powerful, while benefiting from the mystique engendered by the first school to gild inequality and sanctify oppression.
Adrian Hastings

What the Christian citizen has to do in most of his problems concerning the relations of corporate groups of men is to dedicate himself in the power of love to the establishment of justice.

William Temple

We have got so much, we Europeans, but we must realize that we can ultimately renew others only by example.

Laurens van der Post

Look with mercy, O Lord, on the peoples of the world, so sure of their righteousness, and so deeply involved in their unrighteousness.

Reinhold Niebuhr

A scientific and technologically advanced society makes possible a higher standard of living for all, so the attainment of that higher standard tends to become the chief aim, to the exclusion of ethical and spiritual values. In the end that exclusion inevitably leads to the collapse of the society, however technologically advanced it may be; in fact the advanced technology itself may bring about a more rapid and disastrous collapse. There is nothing wrong with a higher standard of living if it is shared by all, but for that to be possible a return to ethical and spiritual values, a return to God, would have to come first. Can we hope to 'turn again'?

I know it is fashionable to say the West is no longer Christian because our churches are emptying fast and our educational institutions are dominated by arid intellectualists who think religion is superstitious and a delinquent state of mind, but western culture is profoundly and incorrigibly Christian, and in its dreaming self preparing to make its established religious self new and contemporary. That is why I think that western man – with all his faults – still has the key to the salvation of the world within his culture, within his philosophy, within his spirit. If only he will go back to its source in his own story he can save not only himself but the world. Western man has the experience – through the experience of empire. He has an experience of eastern, northern and southern as well as western man. In his own context now, in his own heart, he has got so much of the whole world enmeshed, incorporated into the western spirit; his chauvinistic stage is behind him for good, and he has got all the bridges he needs to the rest of the world, if only he will cross them.

Laurens van der Post

If the universe is tending finally to become *something*, how can it keep a place in itself for *Someone*? If the peak of human evolution is regarded as impersonal by nature, the units accepting it will inevitably, in spite of all efforts to the contrary, see their personality diminished under its influence.
Teilhard de Chardin

The type of office or institution usually put up in our time is an impersonal, as it were literal, neutral, structure – akin in its way to the detached, not personally meaningful, business transactions which will take place inside it, each accurately computerised and documented.
Roy Niblett

Our period has decided for a *secular* world. That was a great and much-needed decision. It threw a church from her throne, a church which had become a power of suppression and superstition. It gave consecration and holiness to our daily life and work. Yet it excluded those deep things for which religion stands: the feeling for the inexhaustible mystery of life, the grip of an ultimate meaning of existence, and the invincible power of an unconditional devotion. These things cannot be excluded. If we try to expel them in their divine images, they re-emerge in daemonic images.
Paul Tillich

Restlessness begets meaninglessness, and the lack of meaning in life is a soul-sickness whose full extent and full import our age has not as yet begun to comprehend.
C.G. Jung

As our insensitivity has increased, so naturally our ability to discern our own insensitivity has declined.
  The main route by which society is inwardly enlarged, enriched and cultivated is that of coming to know itself in even greater depth, range and subtlety.
  The main instrument of society's self-knowledge is its culture: culture as a specific field of human activity, influencing the general state of mind – albeit often very indirectly – and at the same time continually subject to its influence.
  A world where 'truth' flourishes not in a dialectic climate of

genuine knowledge, but in a climate of power motives, is a world of mental sterility, petrified dogmas, rigid and unchangeable creeds leading inevitably to creedless despotism.
Vaclav Havel

> O God of earth and altar,
>   Bow down and hear our cry;
> Our earthly rulers falter,
>   Our people drift and die;
> The walls of gold entomb us,
>   The swords of scorn divide,
> Take not thy thunder from us,
>   But take away our pride.
>
> From all that terror teaches,
>   From lies of tongue and pen,
> From all the easy speeches
>   That comfort cruel men,
> From sale and profanation
>   Of honour and the sword,
> From sleep and from damnation,
>   Deliver us, good Lord!

G.K. Chesterton

The certainty that one has found the only true way is a source of strength to the believer. So is the division of the world into the elect and the rejected, which appears in the teaching both of St Augustine and of Calvin. Catholics themselves used to believe that there was no salvation outside the Church.

There is, however, also a gentler form of Puritanism which is very influential among the young in the advanced industrial countries. It is an ideology which links some of the concerns of the Green movement, of the women's movement, of rights for ethnic minorities, with respect for animal life and often, a non-dogmatic spirituality. This ideology tends to reject modern materialism and to cultivate a simple lifestyle, a plain unworldiness which would have been attractive to the plain-living Puritans of New England in the seventeenth century. Many of its adherents are vegetarian. There is more natural Christianity in this ideology than dogma, and the respect for all life has a Franciscan character.

William Rees-Mogg

The biblical account makes human beings responsible for creation to God, and makes it clear that the world is only held in trust by humans. It is post-Newtonian mechanism which deprived creation of any personal basis or goal. Now humans did not hold it on trust for anyone; and they were not bound by any obligations, any objective structures of nature which, having been created by God, humans could not impair. The world is just a purposeless machine; and it can be used in any way that human desires dictate. The technological imperative, the urge to master the environment and subject it to the human will, in turn generates the consumer imperative, which reduces all human transactions to matters of profit and utility. Humanity is master of the machine; it can be made to do whatever humanity wants; and there is no one to hold anyone accountable for their actions.

The fully irreligious view of the natural order is that it is an instrument to be used as one wishes and that there is no objective criterion of what one ought to wish. Of course, since humans themselves are parts of the machine, this leads to treating human beings, too, as objects to be manipulated. Technology, consumerism and colonialism are not connected by accident. They are parts of one process of dehumanization which results when humans believe that they are part of an impersonal machine, and that the most they can do is satisfy as many desires as they happen to have as fully as they possibly can.

Keith Ward

The Holy Spirit, always unsettling, is stirring up his people. He is making them capable of encountering all men and together running to meet the event which will upset all our human calculations and bring life to our dry bones.

Run towards, not away! Run towards mankind's tomorrow, a technological civilization charged with the promise of human development for the poorest.

Run forward to bring new life from within, asking people, exhorting, imploring them, in season and out of season to come together, and so to raise up in the world of men an unmistakable sign of our brotherly love.

Roger Schutz

46

SCIENCE AND RELIGION

A recent opinion poll revealed that, among those people who have doubts about the existence of God, one in three said that the reason was that science had 'disproved' religion.
Russell Stannard

The scientific community is abstractive, for like every community of inquiry it has its own symbolic language by which it represents those aspects of experience in which it is interested. Whitehead warns of the temptation to assume that only those qualities which science can analyze are real:

> The disadvantage of exclusive attention to a group of abstractions, however well-founded, is that by the nature of the case you have abstracted from the remainder of things. Insofar as the excluded things are important to your experience, your modes of thought are not fitted to deal with them.

A symbol-system in which a small group of variables is abstracted can often be very exact, but its representation is likely to be far removed from the complexity and variety of levels of meaning in human experience. The laboratory situation is highly artificial in the sense that it deliberately excludes the 'extraneous influences' that are always present outside the lab. Often the problems most significant to man cannot be analyzed quantitatively or with precision. (For example, it is suggested by Polanyi that historical studies are justified despite their inherent inaccuracy by the intrinsic interest of their subject matter and its breadth of implications; the atom is simple in comparison to the human personality.)
Ian Barbour

Why is it that the elements of reality (science) ignores never come in to disturb it? The reason is that all the terms of physics are defined in terms of one another. The abstractions with which physics begins are all it ever has to do with.
J.W.N. Sullivan

Modern physics is not really concerned with 'things' but with the mathematical relations between certain abstractions which are the residue of the vanished things.
Arthur Koestler

Religion without science is lame, science without religion is blind.
Albert Einstein

Beauty slips through the scientist's net.
John Polkinghorne

> All that I know
>   Of a certain star,
> Is, it can throw
>   (Like the angled spar)
> Now a dart of red,
>   Now a dart of blue,
> Till my friends have said
>   They would fain see, too,
> My star that dartles the red and the blue!
>
> Then it stops like a bird; like a flower,
>   hangs furled:
>   They must solace themselves with
>   the Saturn above it.
> What matter to me if their star is a
>   world?
>   Mine has opened its soul to me;
>   therefore I love it.

Robert Browning

Imagination is more important than knowledge.
Albert Einstein

A popular cliché in philosophy says that science is pure analysis or reductionism, like taking the rainbow to pieces; and art is pure synthesis, putting the rainbow together. This is not so. All imagination begins by analysing nature. Michelangelo said that vividly, by implication, in his sculpture (it is particularly clear in the sculptures that he did not finish) and he also said it explicitly in his sonnets on the act of creation:

> When that which is divine in us doth try
> To shape a face, both brain and hand unite
> To give, from a mere model frail and slight,
> Life to the stone by Art's free energy.

J. Bronowski

The universe begins to look more like a great thought than like a great machine.

James Jeans

The waves that seem to constitute matter . . . are as immaterial as the waves of depression, loyalty, suicide, and so on, that sweep over a country.

J.W.N. Sullivan

You will hardly find one among the profounder sort of scientific minds, without peculiar religious feeling of his own . . . His religious feeling takes the form of rapturous amazement at the harmony of the natural law . . . This feeling is the guiding principle of his life and work. It is beyond question akin to that which has possessed the religious geniuses of all ages.

C.A. Coulson

The myth of creation does not tell us about a first moment of time, any more than the myth of the Fall tells us about a first human being. What it does tell us is that every moment of time, like every contingent thing, comes to be from the creative power of God. The question of the first moment of chronological time is a question for the astrophysicist, not for the theologian, just as the question of the first *Homo sapiens* is a question for the anthropologist, not for the biblical scholar. The event of creation of which we speak in theology is not just

an initial event within a first moment of time; rather it points to the relation of all events to their eternal source.
Langdon Gilkey

When scientists and social scientists discourse about the future of humanity, they are apt to enunciate a view of the human being as moral and rational that is belied by the presuppositions and the conclusions of their scientific studies.
Roy Niblett

It is not the business of science to inherit the earth, but to inherit the moral imagination; because without that man and beliefs and science will perish together.
J. Bronowski

To face up to the totality of what we experience in our environment – both natural objects and human beings – in the act of reflection, is to risk the almost certain chance of being changed.
C.A. Coulson

It was clear that the Pope would not allow the Copernican doctrine to be avowed openly. But there was another way, and the next year Galileo began to write, in Italian, the *Dialogue on the Great World Systems* . . . Galileo put into the book that sense that all his science gives us from the time that, as a young man in Pisa, he had first put his hand on his pulse and watched a pendulum. It is the sense that the laws here on earth reach out into the universe and burst right through the crystal spheres. The forces in the sky are of the same kind as those on earth, that is what Galileo asserts; so that mechanical experiments that we perform here can give us information about the stars. By turning his telescope on the moon, on Jupiter, and the sunspots, he put an end to the classical belief that the heavens are perfect and unchanging, and only the earth is subject to the laws of change.

The book was finished by 1630, and Galileo did not find it easy to get it licensed. The censors were sympathetic, but it soon became clear that there were powerful forces against the book. However, in the end Galileo collected no fewer than four imprimaturs, and early in 1632 the book was published in

Florence. It was an instant success, and for Galileo an instant disaster. Almost at once from Rome the thunder came: Stop the presses. Buy back all the copies – which by then had been sold out. Galileo must come to Rome to answer for it.

J. Bronowski

Post-Galilean science claimed to be a substitute for, or the legitimate successor of, religion; thus its failure to provide the basic answers produced not only intellectual frustration but spiritual starvation.

Arthur Koestler

The basic novelty of our age is the combination of this sudden, unique increase in physical power with an equally unprescedented spiritual ebb-tide.

Arthur Koestler

Technology – that child of modern science, which in turn is a child of modern metaphysics – is out of humanity's control, has ceased to serve us, has enslaved us and compelled us to participate in the preparation of our own destruction.

Vaclav Havel

Man's destiny was no longer determined from 'above' by a super-human wisdom and will, but from 'below' by the sub-human agencies of glands, genes, atoms, or waves of probability. This shift of the locus of destiny was decisive. So long as destiny had operated from a level of the hierarchy higher than man's own, it had not only shaped his fate, but also guided his conscience and imbued his world with meaning and value. The new masters of destiny were placed lower in the scale than the being they controlled; they could determine his fate, but could provide him with no moral guidance, no values and meaning. A puppet of the Gods is a tragic figure, a puppet suspended on his chromosomes is merely grotesque.

Arthur Koestler

The old explanations, with all their arbitrariness and patchiness, answered the question after 'the meaning of life' whereas the new explanations, with all their precision, made the question of meaning itself meaningless.

Arthur Koestler

If it is true, as I think it is, that intelligibility is the ground on which fundamental science ultimately makes its claim to be dealing with the way the world is, then it gives science a strong comradeship with theology, which is engaged in the similar, if more difficult, search for an understanding of God's ways with men.

John Polkinghorne

I have had to learn the lesson that reactions at a microscopic level can have macroscopic results.

Hugh Montefiore

If it is true, as Russell Stannard suggests, that one person in three of those who have doubts about the existence of God believe that science has 'disproved religion' what justification is there for that view?

As Whitehead says in the quotation by Ian Barbour, the abstractions with which science deals inevitably leave a remainder of things important to our experience with which science is not fitted to deal. These things mainly concern the human personality which is not subject to the precise analysis of scientific method. Science, then, is incapable of either proving or disproving the existence of the personal either in man or God.

Yet James Jeans can write that the universe 'begins to look more like a great thought than like a great machine', – and Danah Zohar suggests that human being is a tiny microcosm of cosmic being. Sullivan and Koestler point to the limitations of science undisturbed by a wider 'reality'.

It is a fact that many of the greatest scientists, (Niels Bohr and Albert Einstein are mentioned here), had a religious faith. According to Charles Coulson the scientist's religious feeling 'takes the form of rapturous amazement at the harmony of the natural law'. We must recognise however that this applies only to some even though the greatest. Pierre Duhem demonstrates that there is a close connection between the rise of science and Christian theology and a greater continuity than has previously been accepted. What is absolutely clear (to use the politician's jargon) is that there is no essential conflict, such as is so often assumed, between science and religion.

Pierre Duhem, whose work was deliberately neglected by the anti-clerical establishment in France, demonstrated this both historically and philosophically as the following quotations indicate:

The demolition of Aristotelian physics was not a sudden

collapse; the construction of modern physics did not take place on a terrain where nothing was left standing. From one to the other the passage takes place by a long sequence of partial transformations . . . Those who in the sixteenth century took stock of this substitution of one science for another were seized by a strange illusion. They imagined that this substitution was sudden and that it was their work . . . (they) were celebrated as creators to whom the world owed the renaissance of science. They were very often but continuers and sometimes plagiarizers.

Pierre Duhem

Duhem's demonstration of the importance of medieval thought, and particularly of the close connection between the rise of science and Christian theology, was not welcomed by the anti-clerical establishment of the Third Republic, or by the rationalists and secularists then dominating the historiography of science, and they saw to it that his work was virtually ignored not only during his lifetime but for years after his death.

The work of Duhem is of great relevance today, for it shows clearly the Christian roots of modern science, thus decisively refuting the alleged incompatibility of science and Christianity still propagated by the secularist establishment. Science is an integral part of our Christian culture, a lesson still to be learned even within the Christian Church. From this follows the importance of detailed and accurate scientific studies of many aspects of modern life before any moral judgements are made.

P.E. Hodgson

I'm inclined to think that every really great scientist, every really creative scientist, has some kind of profound religious feeling. Niels Bohr and Albert Einstein were two such scientists in our own time. Einstein used to say, 'What are we doing in science but drawing His lines again?'

Carl von Weizsaecker

The mind/body (mind/brain) duality in man is a reflection of the wave/particle duality which underlies all that is. In this way, human being is a tiny microcosm of cosmic being.

Danah Zohar

The only way to hold together a vital religion and a scientific apprehension of the world is to assert some form of Divine Immanence.

William Temple

Just as there is no space and time between two separate laser beams (their wave patterns interfere across space and time), so there is no real division in space or time between selves. We are all individuals, but individuals within a greater unity, a unity which defines each of us in terms of others and gives each of us a stake in eternity.

We know that quantum physics calls upon us to alter our notions of space and time, but now we have to accept that this touches each and every one of us at the core of our personhood.

Danah Zohar

For those seeking a religious viewpoint, modern physics no longer presents us with the puzzle of a vast machine into which human beings or God do not fit. Instead, it depicts the universe as a vast evolving totality with an inner direction towards richness and complexity of consciousness. Human persons are not alien intrusions in an indifferent machine; they are points of conscious growth in an organic, value-directed process. Values are not subjective matters of individual desire. They are rooted in the nature of things, as that for the sake of which the whole process exists and towards which it strives, the archetypes of being. This is the exciting vision which has supplanted the old mechanistic materialism.

Keith Ward

47

DIFFERENT FAITHS

The boundary between true and false today, even as Christians see it, no longer runs simply *between* Christianity and other religions, but at least in part *within* each of the religions. The principle here is that nothing of value in the other religions is to be denied, but neither is anything of no value to be uncritically accepted ... In short we need a dialogue in *mutual* responsibility and in awareness that none of us possesses the truth 'ready-made', but all are on the way to the 'ever greater' truth.

Hans Küng

Dialogue was not a mere talking about religion; that is very often pure babble, vanity, self-glorification. Nor was dialogue the 'comparative religion' of experts. The comparison of religions is interesting only so long as one has not understood what religion is really all about. One can only compare what lies on the surface – maya. The real dialogue takes place in an ultimate, personal depth: it does not have to be a talking about religion. But something does distinguish real dialogue: the challenge. Dialogue challenges both partners, takes them out of the security of their own prisons their philosophy and theology have built for them, confronts them with reality, with truth: a truth that cannot be carried home black on white, a truth that cannot be left to gather dust in libraries, a truth that demands all ... Dialogue in depth shatters the self-confidence of those who regard themselves as guardians of the whole and only truth. Truth has to be searched for in order to be had; the Kingdom of God is arriving, and only those who are on their way will reach it.

Klaus Klostermaier

I believe that the search for Christ's relevance is a truer and less static way of describing the aim of dialogue than is the older talk about the one word and light which has inspired other religious systems. For it is not in the propositions, regulations, rituals or traditions of a religious system that his universal presence is to be found, but always independent of these phenomena in the uncontainable unattained to which they point, in the questions men ask about them, and the protests men make against them. It is as judge and saviour of the religious tradition itself that Christ's relevance to each religion will be found. It is not so much that he is the culmination or crown of every religion – that is not how I would express it – but that in Him each religion will be brought to fulfilment in terms true to itself, though crisis and conversion.

John Taylor

We can never approach a Christian theology of other religions as though there is anywhere a possibility of getting beyond dispute: there is only the way of disputing creatively and recreatively rather than destructively.

Haddon Willmer

If thankfulness and wonder are indeed the primary element in doctrine about God, then community may be found even where tenets quarrel and perhaps, in measure, even idolatry may be redeemed instead of broken.

Kenneth Cragg

When you see Hindus and Muslims here, when you hear some of them speak of Christ as their brother, then you realize that the mystery of the Church is far vaster than you imagined. You are dumbfounded to discover that those people live an absolute of God with such intensity that we recognise ourselves in them.

Roger Schutz

For God there is neither Hindu nor Muslim.

Guru Nanak
(At a time of conflict between Hindus and Muslims.)

In the depth of every living religion there is a point at which the religion itself loses its importance and that to which it points breaks through its particularity, elevating it to spiritual freedom and with it to a vision of the spiritual presence in other expressions of the ultimate meaning of man's existence.

Paul Tillich

Buber minimised nothing of the contradictions that set Christian and Jew apart. The lines must be drawn not in hatred but love. What was called for was the artist's approach, not commanding but coaxing the form of it into light. It meant being humble enough to rejoice in the otherness of the brother, in the singular otherness to be loved. To the two faiths fell the one task. 'It behoves both you and us to hold inviolably fast to our own true faith, that is to our own deepest relationship to truth. This is not what is called 'tolerance': our task is not to tolerate each other's waywardness but to acknowledge the real relationship in which both stand to the truth. Whenever we both, Christian and Jew, care more for God Himself than for our image of God, we are united in the feeling that our Father's house is differently constructed than our human models take it to be'. The walls of that house do not divide but unite.

Alan Ecclestone

If I differ from you, I don't diminish you, I make you greater.

Antoine de St. Exupéry

Christianity in India should not be an imported, fully fledged and highly developed religion, but Hinduism itself converted – or Islam, or Buddhism, whatever it may be . . . The process of conversion implies a death and resurrection, but, as the risen Christ or the baptised person is the same as previously and yet is a new being, likewise converted Hinduism is the true risen Hinduism, the same and yet renewed, transformed. In one word, the Church brings every true and authentic religion to its fulfilment through a process of death and resurrection which is the true meaning of conversion.

Raymond Pannikar

On the whole, mystical religions seem to have an easier time with tolerance than do religions in which God's prophetic word demands a decision, provokes a 'crisis', and so virtually creates a division between those who listen and those who do not, between the chosen and the not-chosen, and finally between the saved and the damned.

Hans Küng

For Christians the meeting with other Faiths means a radical reassessment of the meaning of mission. 'Conversion' no longer implies leaving one faith system in order to belong to another; it implies a recreation of each faith system from within. As John Taylor says 'It is as judge and saviour of the religious tradition itself that Christ's relevance to each religion will be found'. It is difficult for those of us who have long held the other view to adjust to this new concept of mission. Some will regard it as a betrayal of our own faith. One positive result brought out by Alan Ecclestone must not be over-looked: whereas the traditional idea of mission inevitably led to confrontation between faiths, this one makes possible a move towards mutual understanding and, ultimately, to unity. 'Whenever we . . . care more for God himself than for our image of God, we are united in the feeling that our Father's house is differently constructed than our human models take it to be. The walls of that house do not divide but unite.'

I recognise that the Christian doctrine of the light that lighteth every man demands a reverence for other faiths as being in various ways expressions of the divine wisdom, and I think it right to give practical expression to this reverence for them. On the other hand I do not believe that 'religion' is a kind of banner under which we should all unite as if it contained the essence of what is good versus 'irreligion' as its opposite. Not all religion is good.

Michael Ramsey

Let heart speak to heart, but there must be an engagement of the mind which demands its own asceticism.

Gordon Wakefield

'If you ask him – outstanding guide as he is – to show you what Hinduism or popular Islam are, he responds by telling stories, by introducing you to places and above all to people who have become his friends.' The reason why Roger Hooker responds with stories is that he himself spent thirteen years patiently and receptively waiting and listening to people of many different traditions. He speaks of the need to 'submit ourselves to the patient and humble discipline of listening to others, of being content to spend time with them because God loves them infinitely more than we do. It is only in this context that we can discover how strange and incomprehensible other people find our language, our customs and our beliefs. And it is only when we have made that humiliating, painful and very necessary discovery that we learn that communication is not an automatic process that happens by itself, but an art which has to be learnt, and it is precisely our friends of other faiths who are our teachers in it.'

Kenneth Cracknell
(inner quotes
S. Barrington Ward
Roger Hooker)

O Eternal Word,
   who from the beginning hast revealed
   glimpses of truth and righteousness
   through prophets of many faiths:
We praise Thee
   That all that is of value
     is found fulfilled and perfected in Thee,
   and all that is mistaken
   finds its correction
     in Thee.
Do Thou draw all seekers of truth and righteousness
   to thyself,
and vouchsafe to them the unsearchable riches
   that we have found in Thee, dear Lord.

George Appleton

O God our Father, grant us that openness of heart and mind which will enable us to respect the personality, the customs, the beliefs, the opinions of others, however strange they may be to us. Grant that this openness may be grounded in confidence and trust so that we may not, for fear, be forced to reject those who are different from ourselves.

J.P.

Now may every living thing, young or old, weak or strong, living near or far, known or unknown, living or departed or yet unborn, may every living thing be full of bliss.

The Buddha

48

A CATHOLIC (OR ECUMENICAL) SPIRIT

While (a man of a truly Catholic spirit) is steadily fixed in his religious principles, in what he believes to be the truth as it is in Jesus; while he firmly adheres to that worship of God which he judges to be most acceptable in His sight; and while he is united by the tenderest and closest ties to one particular congregation – his heart is enlarged toward all mankind, those he knows and those he does not; he embraces with strong and cordial affection neighbours and strangers, friends and enemies. This is catholic or universal love. And he that has this is of a catholic spirit for love alone gives the title to this character: catholic love is a catholic spirit.

John Wesley

I must persist in putting it on record that, through a lack of well-grounded information, a lot of people fall into an 'overbearing' style of Christian belief, overbearing and even un-Christian in its absolutist claims, so alien to Jesus and his gospel.

Edward Schillebeeckx

Toleration is not a state or a theory which, once achieved, endures for ever like some principle of human knowledge. It is a principle which each generation has to strive for afresh, in theory as in practice, because even when secured it remains the most precarious of all human achievements.

The faith which attaches the emotions to the rational pursuit of truth in general is no enemy of reason and of tolerance. But that faith which concerns itself with the truth instead of truth, which makes a particular conception of truth an emotional necessity apart from the evidence that has to be considered, is the seed ground of all fanaticism. It is, however, essential that that scepticism which is to assist the cause of tolerance, should remain an intellectual attitude, and not be itself subverted into an emotional conviction. In other words, scepticism must not develop into cynicism, because cynicism is merely fanaticism reversed.

The pursuit of freedom with an intolerant mentality may be self-defeating.

T. Lyon

I think the best and the only way of fulfilling our mission is to sow good seed in good i.e. prepared ground, and not to root up tares where we must inevitably gather all the wheat with them.

George Eliot

The coming generations will have less and less patience with the contradiction of Christians split up into different denominations, with all the energy lost defending opposing viewpoints, at a time when the population explosion is rapidly increasing the number of people with no knowledge of God. They will find it intolerable that the best of Christians' time and energy is going to waste justifying their respective positions.

If Christians seek to be visibly in communion, this is not an end in itself, for a greater sense of ease or for greater power, but so that others may see the truth in them, in order to offer to all men a place of communion where even non-believers feel at ease, under no kind of constraint.

Roger Schutz

He that can apprehend and consider vice with all her baits and seeming pleasures, and yet abstain, and yet distinguish, and yet prefer that which is truly better, he is the true wayfaring Christian.

I cannot praise a fugitive and cloistered virtue, unexercised and unbreathed, that never sallies out and sees her adversary, but slinks out of the race, where that immortal garland is to be run for, not without dust and heat. Assuredly we bring not innocence into the world, we bring impurity much rather; that which purifies us is trial, and trial is by what is contrary.

Since therefore the knowledge and survey of vice is in this

world so necessary to the constituting of human virtue, and the scanning of error to the confirmation of truth, how can we more safely, and with less danger, scout into the regions of sin and falsity than by reading all manner of tractates and hearing all manner of reason? And this is the benefit which may be had of books promiscuously read.

But of the harm that may result hence:

First, is feared the infection that may spread; but then all human learning and controversy in religious points must remove out of the world, yea the Bible itself; for that ofttimes relates blasphemy not nicely, it describes the carnal sense of wicked men not unelegantly, it brings in holiest men passionately murmuring against Providence through all the arguments of Epicurus: in other great disputes it answers dubiously and darkly to the common reader.

John Milton

If I can unite in myself the thought and devotion of Eastern and Western Christendom, the Greek and the Latin Fathers, the Russians and the Spanish mystics, I can prepare in myself the reunion of divided Christians.

From that secret and unspoken unity in myself can eventually come a visible and unspoken unity of all Christians.

If we want to bring together what is divided, we cannot do so by imposing one division upon the other. If we do this, the union is not Christian. It is political and doomed to further conflict.

We must contain all the divided worlds in ourselves and transcend them in Christ.

Thomas Merton

The churches' ecumenical response, while good in itself, is far too slow when compared with the universal wild rush to the abyss.

Alexander Solzhenitsyn

John Wesley's vision of Catholic or universal love is shared by Roger Schutz and Thomas Merton. Roger Schutz applies it to 'Christians split up into different denominations', Thomas Merton to the division within ourselves which must be overcome if we are to contribute to the unity of all Christians. 'We must contain all the divided worlds in ourselves'. John

Milton suggests that this inward unity can be achieved not by escaping from those who differ from us, but by exposing ourselves 'to what is contrary'.

Religions have met before, in conflict and dialogue. What is new today is that we are forced to revise the scriptural infallibilism which characterized past debates. When that is done, new possibilities open up for a global theocentrism which have never existed in the same way before. Our own traditions can be more confidently affirmed as experientially formed symbolic mediations of the infinite, rather than as intellectually established systems of final truth. Is this a possibility for the dispossessed of the great religions, that they may reclaim their homeland without needing to deny the spiritual insights of others?

Keith Ward

One can see in this way how one should not regard 'religions' as monolithic blocks of doctrine which are bound to exclude one another. As such, 'a religion' is no more than a fossilized remnant of a primeval disclosure of the Cosmic Mind in one specific culture. By a creative conversation of traditions, one can gain new insights into the relation of the human and the divine, the finite and the infinite, which are enriching and fruitful for personal prayer, meditation and devotion. One tradition does not have to be rejected, to accept another.

Keith Ward

To be counter-culture to *every* community of exclusion in every idiom of life and speech we can muster – that to me would be the agenda for a decade, no, for a millenium of 'evangelism': a belonging to wrestle with as earth and Kingdom engage.

Elizabeth Templeton

49

HOPE

> I tell you naught for your comfort,
> Yea, naught for your desire,
> Save that the sky grows darker yet
> And the sea rises higher.
> Night shall be thrice night over you,
> And heaven an iron cope
> Do you have joy without a cause,
> Yea, faith without a hope?
>
> G.K. Chesterton

We are left with only the narrow way, a way often hardly to be found of living every day as if it were the last, yet in faith and responsibility living as though a great future still lies before us.
Dietrich Bonhoeffer

> Not, I'll not, carrion comfort, Despair, not feast on thee:
> Not untwist – slack they may be – these last strands of man
> In me or, most weary, cry I can no more, I can;
> Can something, hope, wish day come, not choose not to be.
>
> Gerard Manley Hopkins

Jesus lived for his hope. He did not treat it as something he could adapt to the demands of 'reality'. He subjected 'reality' as well as himself, to it.
Werner & Lotte Pelz

In a Teilhardian theology natural optimism almost merges with supernatural hope. In a Barthian theology, there is an unbridgeable division between the two. Christian hope here says nothing about the foreseeable future of our society. On the contrary, the fall of man and the universal fact of sin should rather persuade us to combine supernatural hope with natural pessimism . . .

Hope distinguishes itself from two temptations, with each of which it does nevertheless have a good deal in common: the optimism which is set on victory now and the pessimism which abandons any expectation of earthly victory at all . . .

Hope is not optimism, but hope is not hope without some optimism. Be a Barthian in reading the signs of the times, but be a Teilhardian still in your equanimity; claim the future. Do not abandon it to the enemy.

To know Christ is not only to know him crucified, whatever the preacher may remark in a moment of enthusiam. It is also to know him as he was in the days of his ministry, upon which the gospels put so much meticulous stress: the experience of welcoming him into one's house, being healed by his word, washing his feet, picnics on the hills, fishing by the lakeside, breaking bread and drinking wine in fellowship. All things of here and now, things of hopefulness, things of joy, things to be remembered and cherished.

Adrian Hastings

It does not seem to occur to us that all this emptiness, all this evidence of breakdown, all this decline in values, this diminishing awareness and sharpened sense of insecurity despite the obvious proliferation of material security in our lives – that all this might be the messenger or the forerunner of something new, and what is knocking at the door should be invited in.

Laurens van der Post

He said that he thought on the whole that life was on the side of meaning as opposed to meaninglessness. He believed in life and he certainly was not despairing. I do not think he would have done what he did in his life if he had been motivated by despair. On the contrary, one of the things about hope is that hope fears all things but at the same time hope ceases not. In

Jung, you see, the hope was strong because love is hope. Love is the hope that ceases not, and ultimately love is certainty.
*Laurens van der Post
on C.G. Jung.*

For if you find hope in the ground of history, you are united with the great prophets who were able to look into the depth of their times, who tried to escape it, because they could not stand the horror of their visions, and who yet had the strength to look to an even deeper level and there to discover hope.
Paul Tillich.

> To suffer woes which Hope thinks infinite;
> To forgive wrongs darker than death or night;
> To defy Power, which seems omnipotent;
> To love, and bear; to hope till Hope creates
> From its own wreck the thing it contemplates;
P.B. Shelley

If hopes were dupes, fears may be liars.
Arthur Hugh Clough

The essential thing is hope, – loss of hope makes for desperate people and desperate people do desperate things.
Rabbi Hugo Gryn

Aaron Marcus began to crossbreed feelings hitherto considered alien and even inimical to each other. The man who privately called himself 'an astronomer of feeling', with modest conceit, attempted, for example, to breed anxiety with hope, or melancholy with longing; in this, it seems, he sought a way to implant every unpleasant, harmful, and destructive feeling with a seed of transcendence, of redemption.
David Grossman

(Abraham) . . . Who against hope believed in hope, that he might become the father of many nations.
Romans 4:18

If it is for this life only that Christ has given us hope, we of all men are most to be pitied.
1 Corinthians 15:19

In thee Lord have I hoped, I shall not be destroyed for ever.
The Te Deum

From Judaism we can all learn:
That God is not very remote but very near. You can speak to him as a parent, friend. That as God constantly creates and renews, so men and women can complete and perfect creation. That the best is yet to come. Ultimately there *will* be universal freedom. That life is really good and should be enjoyed. That it is worth being born. The Jew celebrates life whenever possible.
Rabbi Hugo Gryn

I have tried to follow the supreme shepherd, Jesus Christ, who directed his love to all, but in different ways:
to those dehumanized by anxiety for gain
he showed clearly, out of love, the way to recover
their lost human dignity;
with the poor,
dehumanized outcasts,
he sat at table, also out of love,
to give them hope again.
Oscar Romero

Man is created for hope. For him all things are continually being made new.

In Christ, God made himself poor and hidden. A sign of God cannot be an image which overpowers. God does not ask us to work wonders beyond our means, he wants us simply to understand how to love our brothers.

In these years we can sense a new birth: the People of God on the march towards communion. Prophecy is not dead. Beyond the violence of the present, a new hope is rising.
Roger Schutz

50

LIFE

I have come that men may have life, and may have it in all its fullness.
John 10:10

If you cling to your life you will lose it, but if you give it up for me you will save it.
Matthew 10:39

> Unreal City,
> Under the brown fog of a winter dawn,
> A crowd flowed over London Bridge, so many,
> I had not thought death had undone so many.
T.S. Eliot

The hand of the Lord was upon me, and he brought me out by the Spirit of the Lord, and set me down in the midst of the valley; it was full of bones. And he led me round among them; and behold, there were very many upon the valley; and lo, they were very dry. And he said to me, 'Son of man, can these bones live?' And I answered, 'O Lord God, thou knowest.' Again he said to me, 'Prophesy to these bones, and say to them, O dry bones, hear the word of the Lord. Thus says the Lord God to these bones: Behold, I will cause breath to enter you, and you shall live. And I will lay sinews upon you, and will cause flesh to come upon you, and cover you with skin, and put breath in you, and you shall live; and you shall know that I am the Lord.'
Ezekiel 37. 1–6

By baptism we were buried with him, and lay dead, in order that, as Christ was raised from the dead in the splendour of the Father, so also we might set our feet upon the new path of life.
Romans 6:4

If we are to use the dying to live image we do not refer to any absolute transformation that commitment to Christ has brought or is bringing us but simply to the fact that the life of faith is an affair of growth and continual change. Some of the ways in which we have been conducting our relationships and coping with our anxieties no longer serve us, look as if they were in fact hindering us, as we see our true life now in the figure of Christ. We have a glimpse of the new attitudes we will need to adopt, if only we dare risk them, to further the development of this true life. This change in us is slow but we believe it to be deep. It proceeds through hesitations, failures, pains, small encouragements, occasional tranquil intervals in which life feels to have a fresh breeze blowing through it. There comes a stage of conviction that there is now no going back to that old life of ours . . . We sense the beginning of a freedom, the start of a new loving, that as they intensify may well make that life seem like death, and perhaps we shall use that great language then.

Neville Ward

Real life is meeting.

J.H. Oldham.

Real life cannot be dependent upon the accidents of circumstance, upon comfortable conditions, upon youth or health. It belongs to the category of things that do not pass away. Nor can there be anything superficial about it. It must break forth from the centre of our being.

When I can feel that I am my body and that this does not in any way contradict the fact that I am my mind, then I shall have had experience of resurrection. For it is death which separates and life which unites. To be raised to life, therefore, is to discover that I am *one person*. In the experience of resurrection body and mind are no longer felt to be distinct. They function as a single entity.

H.A. Williams

Life comes from personal involvement and communion with ourselves and our world. But the mental machine is concerned only with intellectual domination and possession.

It kills the living reality in order to analyse it. Analyse a flower petal by petal and there is no flower.

H.A. Williams

Vision, then – the vision without which the people perish – the ability to see people and things as they are – does not come from reducing them to mathematical units which can be manipulated by the calculating mind (the dream of the bureaucrat), but from the involvement and communion which exposes us to disturbance, responsibility and suffering – but which is also the only source of joy.

On reading Niebuhr on Human Nature I was struck by his emphasis upon anxiety as being the normal state of the natural man, – an anxiety arising from his refusal to accept his dependent status in the universe – an anxiety, because of his amazing gift of self-transcendence, to rise to the full height of his stature, anxiety because of his weakness and limitations, not to fall into degradation and meaninglessness. Anxiety to succeed, anxiety not to fail. This anxiety, revealing itself in all kinds of petty worry and fretfulness, self-assertion and pride is the normal inward condition of man.

This anxiety frustrates everything we do and prevents us from achieving the very thing we so anxiously desire. It leads us to assert ourselves by grasping at possessions, at knowledge, at friends, at everything that can bolster up our self-esteem. We become possessive and just because we grasp at things we lose them. This hinders the freedom and spontaneity of our relationships with others because anxiety causes suspicion and mistrust and ties us up in concern about ourselves so that we are not free to enter into the lives and needs of others.

Other kinds of self-knowledge may give us a sense of our own limitations, of our compulsive actions, of our inability to behave in accordance with the dictates of reason, but only this self-knowledge (i.e. the knowledge of ourselves in relationship with a loving God who freely offers himself to us), only this self-knowledge (which some would say involves a sense of sin), leads to a radical change of mind, a repentance, a readiness to abandon self and throw ourselves upon the mercy of God – and to find that faith or trust which drives out fear and brings confidence and strength into our lives.

Creative life is always on the yonder side of convention.

C.G. Jung

The greatest tragedy in theology in the last three centuries has been the divorce of theology from the poet, the dancer, the musician, the painter, the dramatist, the actress, the movie maker.

M.D. Chenn

> Give to me the life I love,
>   Let the lave go by me,
> Give the jolly heaven above
>   And the byway nigh me
> Bed in the bush with stars to see,
>   Bread I dip in the river –
> There's the life for a man like me,
>   There's the life for ever.

R.L. Stevenson

Glory to you for the feast-day of life.

Glory to you for the perfume
of lilies and roses.

Glory to you for each different
taste of berry and fruit.

Glory to you for the sparkling
silver of early morning dew.

Glory to you for the joy
of dawn's awakening.

Glory to you for the new life each day brings.
Glory to you, O God, from age to age.
An Orthodox priest in a Russian prison camp

> I have life before me still
> And thy purpose to fulfil;
> Yea a debt to pay thee yet:
> Help me, Sir, and so I will.
> *Gerard Manley Hopkins*

Being a religion of love (Christianity) must indeed see all isolation, whether of misunderstanding or guilt or resentment, as part of the wrongness of life. Accordingly, its view of the fulfilment of life is in community terms, as an ultimate fellowship of loving in which all men and things are loved in the love of God, not the love that excludes because it is the intense predilection of one person for another, of one person for some part of reality, but the loving that is simply the way all will live and have their being.

Neville Ward

Why should I let the toad *work*
  Squat on my life?
Can't I use my wit as a pitchfork
  And drive the brute off?

Six days of the week it soils
  With its sickening poison –
Just for paying a few bills!
  That's out of proportion

Ah were I courageous enough
  To shout *Stuff your pension!*
But I know, all too well, that's the stuff
  That dreams are made on:

For something sufficiently toad-like
  Squats in me, too;
Its hunkers are heavy as hard luck,
  And cold as snow,

And will never allow me to blarney
  My way to getting
The fame and the girl and the money
  All at one sitting.

  I don't say, one bodies the other
    One's spiritual truth;
  But I do say it's hard to lose either,
    When you have both.

Philip Larkin

Everyone suddenly burst out singing;
And I was filled with such delight
As prisoned birds must find in freedom,
Winging wildly across the white
Orchards and dark-green fields; on – on – and out of sight

Everyone's voice was suddenly lifted;
And beauty came like the setting sun:
My heart was shaken with tears; and horror

Drifted away . . . O, but Everyone
Was a bird; and the song was wordless; the singing will never
   be done.

Siegfried Sassoon

I will give unto him that is athirst of the fountain of the water of life freely.

Revelation 21:6

BIBLICAL REFERENCES

Glossary

RSV	Revised Standard Version
AV	Authorised Version
FPJW	Forms of Prayer for Jewish Worship
JB	Jerusalem Bible
BCP	Book of Common Prayer
NIV	New International Version
NEB	New English Bible
LB	Living Bible

Page No	Quotation	Version
20	Acts 17:28	RSV
27	Psalm 127:1	AV
28	Psalm 130:5,6	FPJW
32	Psalm 46:10	RSV
42	Luke 10:41–42	JB
52	John 3:16	RSV
53	Matthew 23:37	JB
57	Psalm 42:1a	BCP
58	Jeremiah 31:33(a)	NIV
58	1 John 4:20	NEB
62	John 1:14	NEB
71	Luke 23:46	NEB
90	John 8:32	RSV
90	John 15:26	RSV
94	Ephesians 4:15	RSV
105	Luke 24:25–27	RSV
113	Luke 18:10–14	RSV
116	Deuteronomy 30:19	RSV
116	Matthew 25:42–45	RSV
118	Matthew 21:28	RSV
118	Matthew 7:1	RSV
120	Matthew 18:21–22	RSV
122	Psalm 103	FPJW
123	Luke 7:47	RSV

133	Hebrews 11:8,10	AV
136	Mark 9:24	AV
137	Matthew 8:8	Adapted (Tridentine Mass)
139	Matthew 18:3	RSV
139	Magnificat Luke 1:51–52	BCP
155	Matthew 5:43–45	RSV
159	Luke 23:34	RSV
160	Psalm 43:4	Vulgate
161	Luke 2:10	AV
162	Psalm 100:1–2	FPJW
162	Isaiah 52:9	AV
162	Hebrews 12:1	AV
162	Psalm 84:4–7	FPJW
163	Galatians 5:22	NEB
165	Romans 14:17	NEB
165	Hebrews 12:14	NEB
165	Ephesians 2:14	NEB
175	Psalm 55:12–15	BCP
176	Ecclesiasticus 25:1	JB
176	John 15:15	RSV
176	John 15:13	AV
177	2 Corinthians 9:7	RSV
177	Acts 20:35	RSV
178	Matthew 5:42	RSV
178	Luke 6:38	RSV
178	Mark 12:41–44	NEB
179	Tobit 4:8	The Apocrypha Revised Version 1894
180	Genesis 18:1–5	NEB
180	Hebrew 13:2	RSV
182	Psalm 116	FPJW
183	Psalm 95:1	BCP
186	Matthew 16:25	NEB
188	Romans 12:2	RSV
190	1 Corinthians 1:27	NIV
193	Job 2:13	NEB
195	Revelation 7:13–17	NIV
203	Galatians 2:20	AV
206	Matthew 18:1–3	JB
216	Mark 10:16	NEB
217	Exodus 13:3	NEB
217	Galatians 5:1	NEB
217	1 Peter 2:16	NEB
221	Mark 10:27	NIV
222	Exodus 14:10–13	NEB
228	Galatians 3:28	NIV
259	Romans 4:18	AV
259	1 Corinthians 15:19	NEB

261	John 10:10	NEB
261	Matthew 10:39	LB
261	Ezekiel 37 1–6	RSV
261	Romans 6:4	NEB
267	Revelation 21:6	AV

INDEX OF AUTHORS QUOTED

	Page No.	Source
Abelard	93	*Sic et Non*
Abishikta Nanda	21, 38–9	*Prayer*
À Kempis	157	*The Imitation of Christ*
Amiel	85, 203	*Journal Intime*
Appleton	252	*The Oxford Book of Prayer*
Aquinas	145, 174	*Summa Theologica*
Arendt	196	*Eichmann in Jerusalem*
Arnold	135	*The Scholar Gypsy*
Auden	56, 89, 162, 194, 226	*Collected Poems*
	115	quoted in Fox, *Original Blessing*
Augustine of Hippo	21, 56	*De Civitate Dei*
	145	*De Moribus Ecclesiae*
	173	*Sermons*
	173	*Confessions*
Baeck	188	Written in 1944 in Theresienstadt concentration camp
Baillie	59, 120	*God was in Christ*
Baker	95	*The Foolishness of God*
Barbour	240	*Issues in Science and Religion*
Barrington Ward	252	quoted in Cracknell, *Towards a New Relationship*
Barry	72	*What has Christianity to Say?*
	120	*Christian Ethics and Secular Society*
Barth	26, 117, 133	*Epistle to the Romans*
Batra	177	quoted in *Forms of Prayer for Jewish Worship*
Beeching	183	*Prayers*
Benson	32	*The Theresian Contemplative*
Berdyaev	104–5, 221	*Freedom and the Spirit*
Bhagavadgita	74	
Blake	32, 46, 104, 110, 121, 122, 146, 160, 161, 174, 175, 208	*Blakes's Poetry and Prose*
	56	quoted in *The Faith of a Moralist*

	Page No.	Source
	90	*Notebooks (1800–1803)*
Bloom A.	184	quoted in Priestland, *Priestland's Progress*
Bloom W.	25	*The New Age*
Bloy	149	*Letter to his Fiancée*
Boff	97, 107, 109, 182, 189–90, 224	*Church, Charism and Power*
Böll	57	Texts for Havel *Living in Truth*
Bonhoeffer	19, 150–1	*Life Together*
	26	*The Confessing Church*
	91, 141–2, 156, 194, 198, 204, 257	*The Cost of Discipleship*
Boros	140, 153, 163, 194–5	*Open Spirit*
	69	Untraced
Braque	88	quoted in Edward Robinson, *The Language of Mystery*
Braybrooke	149–50, 219	*Time to Meet*
Bridges	85	based on Paulus Gerhardt
Bronowski	242, 243, 243–4	*The Ascent of Man*
Brown P.	182	*Augustine of Hippo*
Brown R. E.	61	quoted in Robinson. *The Priority of John*
	63	quoted in Braybrooke, *Time to Meet*
Browning	67, 117, 131–2, 134, 205, 241	*The Poems of Robert Browning*
Bryant (SSJE)	44, 45	letter to Author
Buber	35, 66	*I and Thou*
Buddha	94, 252	
Bultman	182	untraced
Bunyan	140	*Hymns and Psalms*
	204	*The Pilgrim's Progress*
Butterfield	155–6	*History and Human Relations*
	208	*Christianity and History*
Byers	136	quoted in James *A Life of Bishop John A. T. Robinson*
Byrom	55	in *Oxford Book of Christian Verse*
Campbell	102, 207	BBC Broadcast, Aug. 1990
Camus	118	*La Chute*
Chandernagor	235	*La Sans Pareille*
Chapman	18, 39, 229–30	*Spiritual Letters*
Chasidic	49	quoted in *Forms of Prayer for Jewish Worship*
Chateaubriand	43	*La Réponse du Seigneur*
Chenn	264	quoted in Fox, *Original Blessing*

	Page No.	Source
Chesterton	238, 257	*Collected Poems*
Clough	259	*Oxford Book of English Verse*
Coleridge	51	*The Ancient Mariner*
	71	*The Young Coleridge*
	91	*Aids to Reflection*
Coulson	138, 242, 243	*Science and Chriistian Belief*
Coventry	134	article in *The Gospel and Our Culture*
Cracknell	135, 251–2	*Towards a New Relationship*
Cragg	168	*Alive to God*
	181, 249	*The Mind of the Qu'ran*
Craig	158	*Candles in the Dark*
Crashaw	199	*Hymn to St. Theresa*
Cruickshank	98, 99	Untraced
Cupitt	87, 96, 98, 104, 207	*Radicals and the Future of the Church*
Dante	50	*Paradiso*
Davis	77	*Every Day God*
Dawes	98	*Theology* March/April 1990.
De Caussade	34, 42–3, 210, 229	*Abandonment to Divine Providence*
De Mello	45	*The Song of the Bird*
	230	*Sadhana, A Way to God*
Dodd	59, 100	*The Authority of the Bible*
Donne	70–1, 77, 121	*Complete Poetry, and Selected Prose*
Dostoyevsky	93	quoted in Weatherhead, *The Christian Agnostic*
	220–1	*The Brothers Karamazov*
Duhem	245–6	*The Structure of the World*
Dumitrio	24–5	untraced
Ecclestone	97, 250	*The Night Sky of the Lord*
Eckhart	31, 112	quoted in Gollancz *A Year of Grace*
	53, 89	quoted in Fox, *Original Blessing*
	183	Fox, *Meditations with Meister Eckhart*
	209	untraced
Einstein	209, 241	quoted in *At Home on Planet Earth*
Eliot G.	69	*Adam Bede*
	86	*Daniel Deronda*
	144	*Romola*
	151	*Felix Holt*
	226, 254	quoted in Uglow, *George Eliot*
Eliot T. S.	31, 228	*The Rock*
	37, 40, 118	*Little Gidding*
	81	*Journey of the Magi*
	113, 114, 166, 197	*Murder in the Cathedral*

	Page No.	Source
	261	*A Game of Chess*
Elliott C.	225	*Praying the Kingdom*
Emerson	93	quoted in Weatherhead, *The Christian Agnostic*
Flecker	85	*Hassan*
Fox	88, 150, 194, 234	*Original Blessing*
Fromm	77, 205–6, 218–9	*The Fear of Freedom*
	145, 152	*The Art of Loving*
Fynn	206	*Mister God This is Anna*
Gandhi	63	*What Jesus Means to Me*
Gerhardt	85	*Hymn at Nightfall*, Robert Bridges
Gilkey	242	*Maker of Heaven and Earth*
Glover	63	*The Conflict of Religions in the Early Roman Empire*
Goethe	88	quoted in van der Post, *A Walk with a White Bushman*
Goldsmith	174	*The Good-Natured Man*
Graham	30	*The Faith of a Quaker*
Greene	96	quoted in *The Spectator* 18.4.1981
Gregory	203–4	untraced
Griffiths Dom B.	59, 103, 150	*The Golden String*
	60	quoted in *C. S. Lewis at the Breakfast Table*
Griffith-Jones	102	*The Bible, Its Meaning and Aim*
Grimsley	184	*Kierkegaard*
Grossman	112, 190, 193, 259	*See Under: Love*
	88	*R.E. Today* Spring '87
Gryn	259	From BBC *The Moral Maze*
Guardini	142	*The Life of Faith*
Habgood	89	Sermon preached in Ripon Cathedral at the Northern Choirs Festival
Hammerskjold	32, 39, 71, 81, 168, 230	*Markings*
Harries	193	Unpublished paper
	227	Thought for the Day 13.10.1989
Hastings	98, 108, 235, 257–8	*In the Hurricane*
Havel	24, 65, 139–40	Speech on acceptance of Peace Prize in Germany, October 1989
	91–2, 93, 186,	*Living in Truth*

	Page No.	**Source**
	190, 197, 210, 225, 234, 237–8, 244	
Herbert	41, 52, 58, 229	*The Poems of George Herbert*
Hick	60, 64	*God in the Universe of Faiths*
Hildegard of Bingen	81–2	quoted in Bowie and Davies, *Hildegard of Bingen*
Hilton	199	Article in *The Independent Magazine*, 3rd August, 1991
Hodgson	193	*The Doctrine of Atonement*
	246	quoted in Occasional Paper, Farmington Institute
Hooker	251–2	quoted in Cracknell, *Towards a New Relationship*
Hopkins G. M.	30	*The Habit of Perfection*
	51	*God's Grandeur* (Poems 1876–1889)
	163–4	*Spring*
	257	*Carrion Comfort*
	265	*Poems and Prose*
Houlden	65, 93	*Patterns of Faith*
Hoyland	31	*The Fourfold Sacrament*
Hügel	26	*Essays and Addresses*
	56, 139,	*Selected Letters*
	68, 78	*Letters to a Niece*
Hughes	75, 107, 108, 111–112, 112, 138, 163, 179	*God of Surprises*
Huxley	56	*The Perennial Philosophy*
Hylton	112	*The Seal of Perfection*
Jacobs	133	quoted in *Forms of Prayer for Jewish Worship*
James	209	*Varieties of Religious Expericence*
Jeans	242	*The Mysterious Universe*
Jenkins	137–8	*Beyond Religion*
John of the Cross	42	*The Spiritual Canticle*
John Paul II	211	at Assisi for the World Day of Prayer for Peace 1986
Johnson	174	quoted in Boswell, *The Life of Samuel Johnson*
Jones	100–1	quoted in S. Prickett, *Words and the Word*
Jonson B.	175	*Cynthia's Revels*
Julian of Norwich	57, 126, 136, 137, 189	*Revelations of Divine Love*
Jung	24, 31, 146	quoted in van der Post, *A Walk with a White Bushman*
	78, 113	*Modern Man in Search of a Soul*

	Page No.	Source
	213, 264	*The Integration of the Personality*
	237	quoted in Norman, *Silence in God*
Kagawa	19	*Meditations*
King	168	
	198–9, 222	quoted in Craig, *Candles in the Dark*
Kirkegaard	39	quoted in *The Oxford Book of Prayer*
Klostermaier	248	*Hindu and Christian in Urindaban*
Koestler	241, 244	*The Sleepwalkers*
Kraemer	78	*The Christian Message in a Non-Christian World*
Küng	22, 69, 191–2	*Eternal Life*
	30	*Does God Exist?*
	61, 64–5, 72, 116, 121, 124–6, 131	*On Being A Christian*
	114, 217	untraced
	248	*Christianity and the World Religions*
Larkin	95–6	*Church Going*
	266	*Toads*
Lawrence	40, 42	*The Practice of the Presence of God*
Levi	176	*The Mirror Maker*
Lewis	103	untraced
Lyon	253–4	*The Theory of Religious Liberty in England*
Lyward	178	Unpublished paper
	212	Article in *Mental Hygiene*, October 1936
	212	Article in *Children's Communities* October 1944
	212–3	Untraced
Macauley	219	*Literary Essays* in the *Edinburgh Review* August 1825
Machiavelli	226	*The Prince*
Macneice	222–3	*Prayer before Birth*
Maimonides	177	quoted in *Forms of Prayer for Jewish Worship*
Main	45, 230	*The Way of Unknowing*
Marcel	164	*Being and Having*
Maritain J.	34–5	*Les Degrés du Savoir*
	165	*Introduction to Philosophy*
Maritain R.	191	*Les Grandes Amitiés*
Marti	75–6	quoted in Küng, *Eternal Life*
Matheson	221	*Hymns and Psalms*
Mauriac	35	*La Pharisienne*
Maurice	102	*Lectures on the Epistle to the Hebrews*

	Page No.	**Source**
Maurois	114	*A History of France*
Mechtild of Magdeburg	176	quoted in Fox, *Original Blessing*
Meir	40	quoted in Gollancz, *A Year of Grace*
Mendel	138	quoted in Gollancz, *A Year of Grace*
Merton	31	Prayer to his patroness, Our Lady of Carmel
	50 ?	
	134?	
	231	The Cell
	255?	
Meynell	66	*God in the Universe*
Milton	254–5	*Areopagitica*
Montefiore	245	*The Probability of God*
Montgomery	71	*The Methodist Hymn Book*
Moran	104, 215–6	*God Still Speaks*
More	157	quoted in *The Oxford Book of Prayer*
Morgan	154	untraced
Moule	72	*The Origin of Christology*
Murdoch	43–4, 56, 86, 146–7, 175	*The Sovereignty of Good*
Murray	203	*Life in Jesus*
Nanak	249	quoted by Indarjit Singh, Thought for the Day 3rd July, 1990
Newbigin	124	*The Household of God*
	133	*The Other Side of 1984*
	181	*Christian Freedom in the Modern World*
Niblett	134, 237, 243	*Audenshaw Paper No. 126*
Nicholl	215	*Holiness*
Niebuhr	236	untraced
Nikaya	158–9	untraced
Norman	32	*Silence in God*
Nouwen	153	*Seeds of Hope*
Noyes	17	*Art, the Herald*
Oldham	93–4	*Life is Commitment*
	262	quoted in Neil, *Concise Dictionary of Religious Quotations*
Oman	114, 122, 135, 142	*Grace and Personality*
Oppenheimer	109	*Theology* (March/April 1990)
Orthodox Priest	263	in a Russian Prison Camp
O'Shaughnessy	89	*Ode*
Oz	158	quoted by Friedland, *Independent* 9th February, 1991
Pannikar	250	Article in *Christian Revelation and World Religions*

	Page No.	Source
Pascal	22, 30, 70, 127	*Pensées*
Pasternak	65–6, 208	*Doctor Zhivago*
Patmore	153	*The Rod, The Root and the Flower*
	181	*Amelia*
Pelz	146, 185, 257	*God is No More*
Plowman	110–11	*Introduction to the Study of Blake*
Polkinghorne	196	*The Way the World Is*
Popieluszko	196	quoted in Sirkorska, *A Martyr for the Truth*
Prickett J.	252	Unpublished prayer
Prickett S.	101, 109	*Words and the Word*
	160	*Coleridge and Wordsworth*
Prickett W. E.	141	Letter to Raymond George
Qur'an	117	*Surah of the Land*
Rahner	45–6, 106, 173	*Opportunities for Faith*
Raleigh	164	*The Passionate Man's Pilgrimage*
Ramsey	62, 190	*Gateway to God*
	92, 92–3	*The Gospel and the Catholic Church*
	251	quoted in Chadwick, *Michael Ramsey, A Life*
Rauschning	21, 70	*The Beast from the Abyss*
Rees-Mogg	238	article in *The Independent*, 31st December, 1990
Robinson E.	27, 87, 88, 103, 136, 142–3, 210–211, 215	*The Language of Mystery*
Robinson J. A. T.	20, 60, 61, 66–7, 108, 150, 151, 190	quoted in James, *A Life of Bishop J. A. T. Robinson*
	23?	
	36, 40, 45	*Honest to God*
	66	*The Priority of John*
Romero	99, 167, 185, 189, 260	*The Church is All of You*
Rumi	113	*The Masuavi*
Ruskin	94	quoted in Weatherhead, *The Christian Agnostic*
Russell	22	*Autobiography*
	165	*What I Believe*
	234	on Joseph Conrad
Saint-Exupéry	46, 117	*Pilote de Guerre*
	73, 186, 189	*Terre des Hommes*
	250?	
St. Mary's Abbey	29, 33	
Sales, St. Francis de	39	*Introduction to the Devout Life*

	Page No.	**Source**
Sassoon	25	*Collected Poems* 1908–1956
	32?	
	266–7	Selected Poems?
Sartre	221	untraced
Sayers	121	*Unpopular Opinions*
Schillebeeckx	61, 79	*Jesus*
	60	untraced
	72–3, 166	*God Among Us*
	79, 161, 209, 226, 227 253?	*Christ*
Schopenhauer	22, 93	*Essays*
Schutz	28, 41, 49, 97–8, 152, 178, 185, 239, 249, 254, 260	quoted in Brico, *Taizé*
Schweitzer	151	*My Life and Thought*
Shakespeare	40	*The Tempest*
	70, 152, 174	*Sonnets*
	123	*The Merchant of Venice*
	175	*As You Like It*
Shaw	160	*Man and Superman*
Shelley	194	*Julian and Maddalo*
	259	*Prometheus Unbound*
Shemariah	167?	
Simon	132	*Story and Faith*
Sobrino	43	article in *Concilium*, March 1983
Soelle	75	*Suffering*, quoted in Craig, *Candles in the Dark*
Solzhenitsyn	116, 234, 255	Speech at Guildhall, 10th May 1983
Stannard	240	in *At Home on Planet Earth*
Steinberg	69	quoted in *Forms of Prayer for Jewish Worship*
Stevenson	264	*The Vagabond*
Streeter	120, 188–9	*Reality*
Sullivan	241, 242	quoted in Koestler, *The Sleepwalkers*
Swinburne	183	*Ave atque Vale*
Tagore	161	quoted in *Forms of Prayer for Jewish Worship*
Tanner	214	*Double Harness*
Tawney	145	quoted in B.B.C. talk by Daniel Jenkins
Taylor	99, 235	*Oxford Illustrated History of Christianity*
	249	*The Go-Between God*
Teilhard de Chardin	17, 18, 36, 68	*Le Milieu Divin*
	24, 36	*Lettre à un Ami*

	Page No.	Source
	68	*Hymn of the Universe*
	115	*On Suffering*
	144	*Letter to Marguerite*, 20th April, 1919
	154	quoted in Andrews, *The Art and Practice of Loving*
	149, 237	*On Love*
Temple	40	*Christus Veritas*
	46, 61, 98, 106, 109, 175	*Readings in St. John's Gospel*
	131, 133	*Mens Creatrix*
	148?	
	165?	
	213–4?	
	235–6	*Christianity and Social Order*
	247	quoted in Montefiore, *The Probability of God*
Templeton	256	Address to W.C.C., Canberra, February 1991
Terence	209	untraced
Theragatha	142	*Pali Canon*, Psalm 32
Thérèse de Lisieux	32	untraced
Thich Nhat Hanh	229	*Being Peace*
Thomas D.	69	*Collected Poems 1934–1952*
Thomas R. S.	28	*Selected Poems 1946–1968*
Thompson	50	*The Hound of Heaven*
	113	*Health and Holiness*
Tillich	27, 126, 237, 259	*The Shaking of the Foundations*
	249–50	*Christianity and the Encounter of World Religions*
Tournier	166	*The Strong and the Weak*
Toynbee	191	*Towards Holy Spirit*
Traherne	164	*The Salutation*
Twain	146	quoted in Pelz, *God is No More*
Uglow	87	*George Eliot*
Unamuno	93	*La Agonia del Christianismo*
	191	quoted in Judeth M. Brown, *Men and Gods in a Changing World*
Underhill	36	*Letters*
	211	*Immanence*
Van der Post	23, 80–1, 102, 228, 236, 258, 258–9	*A Walk with a White Bushman*
Van Gogh	55	*A Self-Portrait, Letters Revealing his Life as a Painter*
	89	*Letter to Leo*

	Page No.	Source
Vann	137	*The Divine Pity*
Vanstone	214	*Love's Endeavour, Love Expense*
Vatican II	97	*The Church in the Modern World*
Verghese	27, 235	Address given at Conference of European Churches, Nyborn, Denmark, October 1962
Verney	53, 60–1, 70, 101–2, 118, 151	*Water into Wine*
Von Weizsaecker	246	On receiving Templeton Prize 1989
Wakefield	251	*A Dictionary of Christian Spirituality*
Walesa	166	to a French journalist in Paris, September 1981
	196	quoted in *The Times*
Ward K.	67, 92, 99, 123, 144, 239, 247, 256	*A Vision to Pursue*
Ward N.	41, 90, 134, 229, 262, 265	*Five for Sorrow, Ten for Joy*
	73, 152, 194	*Friday Afternoon*
Weil	22, 41, 51, 62, 90, 91, 96, 124, 141, 146, 173, 215	*Attente de Dieu*
	79	*La Pesanteur et la Grâce*
Wesley C.	138	*Hymns and Psalms*
Wesley J.	17, 80, 178, 253	*Forty-Four Sermons*
	121	*Journal*, 24th May, 1738
White P.	19	*Riders in the Chariot*
	113	quoted in an obituary, *The Independent*, 2nd October, 1990
White V.	36	*God and the Unconscious*
Whitehead	53	*Science and the Modern World*
Wilde	74–5	*De Profundis*
	122	*A Woman of No Importance*
Williams	75, 79, 79–80, 80, 106–7, 262, 263	*True Resurrection*
	132	*Soundings*
	79	*The True Wilderness*
Willmer	249	quoted in Moule, *The Origin of Christology*
Wilson	160	untraced
Yeats	176	*The Municipal Gallery Revisited*
Yerushalmi	160	quoted in *Forms of Prayer for Jewish Worship*

	Page No.	**Source**
Yebamot	193	quoted in *Forms of Prayer for Jewish Worship*
Zahrnt	131	untraced
Zohar	246, 247	*The Quantum Self*
Zunz	193	quoted in *Forms of Prayer for Jewish Worship*